/F68.

F
68
.G5
197

Date Due

DISCARD

Morton Grove, Illinois

THE ENGLISHMAN IN KANSAS

THE
ENGLISHMAN
IN KANSAS

or

SQUATTER LIFE AND BORDER WARFARE

BY T. H. GLADSTONE

Introduction by Frederick Law Olmsted
Foreword by James A. Rawley

UNIVERSITY OF NEBRASKA PRESS · LINCOLN

International Standard Book Number 0-8032-0800-6

Library of Congress Catalog Card Number 74-155700

The introduction and text of this edition are reproduced from
the 1857 edition, published by Miller & Company, New York,
through the courtesy of the Kansas State Historical Society.

Manufactured in the United States of America

CONTENTS

FOREWORD

———

"An honest contemporary narrative," pronounced the historian Samuel Eliot Morison of Thomas H. Gladstone's *The Englishman in Kansas.* He went on to observe that most accounts of the struggle for Kansas are "grossly partisan." Honesty and absence of partisanship were qualities hard to find in the mid–1850s as the Union seethed with excitement over the Kansas imbroglio. From the pens of contemporaries—newspapermen and emigrants—the public of the antebellum decade read shrill polemics that doubtless shaped their crucial decisions for secession, no compromise, and war in the secession winter of 1860–1861. The press—North and South—engaged in what a later generation termed "yellow journalism." A saturnalia of partisanship, sectionalism, moralizing, and defamation set in.

An outsider's perspective, therefore, is welcome. The eye and ear of a foreign reporter who had not been brought up amidst the American quarrel over slavery deserve an audience. All the better if he should be a staff member of perhaps the most renowned newspaper in the English-speaking world. And better yet, if before surveying the sectional strife on the western prairie, he had traveled in the Eastern and Southern states.

Thomas H. Gladstone, a kinsman of the eminent English statesman, William Ewart Gladstone, came to the United States in 1856, accompanying John T. Delane, the editor of *The Times*—the mighty London newspaper known as "The Thunderer." The junior correspondent had a driving curiosity about the Kansas question, which as he tells us, seemed buried beneath "a mass of contradictory assertions." In New York City, where journalism was perhaps yellowest, in the late winter of 1855–56 he noted "strange differences" between what the public journals related and what the president reported. In Washington he saw two rival delegates, each claiming to represent the people of Kansas Territory. And in the Congress he saw a legislative stalemate, resulting in the decision to

send a fact-finding committee to investigate reports
of troubles in the territory. Finding press, president,
and lawmakers in sharp disagreement, the puzzled
Englishman resolved to go to Kansas to learn where
the truth lay.

After having been steeped in Southern views of
the violent controversy for two or three months,
he arrived in Lawrence, Kansas, the day after it
had been sacked by Missouri "Border Ruffians" and
Kansas proslavery men. The Free State Hotel had
been burned, homes of freestate men pillaged, the
offices and presses of *The Herald of Freedom* and
The Kansas Free State destroyed. Set on a course
of violence, Kansas began to "bleed," and an eager,
partisan press kindled emotions North and South.

For five years Kansas dominated American politics. The titanic controversy erupted in 1854 when
Congress, under the leadership of Senator Stephen
A. Douglas, rash about means to promote western
development, repealed the thirty-four year old Missouri Compromise. The statesmen of 1820 had "for-
ever prohibited" slavery in the vast inland empire
lying north of the line 36°30′ between the Missouri
River and the Rocky Mountains. The politicians of
1854, after voiding the Compromise of 1820, had

left the people of the territory free to establish or prohibit slavery.

Irate antislavery Congressmen forthwith attacked repeal "as a gross violation of a sacred pledge," and Northern resistance to the extension of Negro slavery endured until the irrepressible conflict split the republic in 1861. Believers in using the power of the national government to thwart the spread of slavery formed the Republican party and took their stand against the Democrats, who were committed to Douglas's popular sovereignty. The Douglas doctrine intrusted the fate of the territory to its settlers. The Democratic president, Franklin Pierce, a friend of minimal government, appeared to think he had acquitted himself of his executive responsibilities in appointing Andrew H. Reeder of Pennsylvania as the first territorial governor.

The "Kansas Question" sharpened as the scramble for Kansas commenced. The newly organized territory, with its rich lands, nearness to river transport, and sparkling future—especially when a transcontinental railroad should have been built—lay immediately west of slaveholding Missouri. For Missourians, Kansas Territory offered the prospect both of prosperity to their economy and peril to their society. Farmlands, townsites, trade opportunities, government contracts, and political posts were among the material advantages beckoning men west. Northern settlers, intent on prohibiting Negro slavery, posed the threat of establishing a free state which might undermine slavery in Missouri. The western counties of Missouri, bordering the new territory and holding the bulk of the state's slaves, had a vital stake in the future of Kansas.

Aggravating the situation, in alarmed Missourians minds, was the organization of a New England Emigrant Aid Company to assist westering pioneers. Backed by the Massachusetts philanthropist Amos Lawrence (for whom the Kansas town was named) and others, it encouraged freestate settlers; and its officers in the course of time armed some settlers with Sharps rifles. This enterprise—centering in Massachusetts, already hated for its abolitionism— though it furnished few settlers, furnished a pretext for Missourians to intervene in Kansas affairs, and provoked Southerners to send expeditions of settlers and swashbucklers to the territory.

When in the autumn of 1854 a territorial delegate to Congress was to be chosen, about seventeen hundred armed men from western Missouri crossed the river and voted in the elections. Amidst scenes of violence and fraud the proslavery candidate, John W. Whitfield, was elected. To the dismay of many Northerners, popular sovereignty was prostituted in like manner in March 1855. In the election of a territorial legislature, some five thousand "Border Ruffians," led by Missouri's coarse-grained Senator David Atchison, intruded and stuffed ballot boxes. Governor Reeder threw out a few of the fraudulent returns, and in a tense scene, while armed men looked on, he accepted most of the results from districts, he said, where no complaints had been filed.

The legislators' meeting at Shawnee Mission on the Missouri border, purged their numbers of its freestate members, and enacted a set of notorious laws. Branded by Northern critics as the "bogus legislature," it established slavery in territorial law, excluded antislavery men from officeholding by means of a test oath, and as part of a Draconian slave code decreed that persons who denied the legal existence of slavery in the territory could be sentenced to imprisonment at hard labor.

Antislavery settlers in angry response repudiated the Shawnee laws and demanded admission to the

Union as a free state. Meeting at Topeka they devised a government that prohibited both slavery and free Negroes. Approval by freestate voters in December 1855 presented the territory with antagonistic governments—proslavery and antislavery.

Earlier, in July, Pierce had removed Reeder and replaced him with a proslavery governor, Wilson Shannon. The freestate men named Reeder their delegate to Congress, a rival to the proslavery representative Whitfield. They elected Charles Robinson, who had been an agent of the emigrant aid company, governor.

At the opening of the year 1856 Pierce showed his sympathies for the Shawnee government by renouncing the Topeka government. Congress then took a hand, and unable to choose between Shawnee and Topeka, as Democrats and Republicans lined up behind the opposing factions, the House named a three-man committee to investigate fraud in the Kansas elections and report. The House committee and Thomas H. Gladstone were in Kansas in the spring of 1856.

Gladstone first published his impressions in *The Times*. One of his articles figured in the presidential election. It was his graphic depiction of the "Border

Ruffians," violent, vulgar, ardent, and rowdy men of the frontier who forced themselves upon Kansas affairs. The Englishman's article was taken up by the freesoil press, and used with telling effect in the Republican attempt to make John C. Frémont president on the Kansas issue. Gladstone's method, he tells us, was to gather his testimony, for the most part, from proslavery men. "I have endeavored to omit all statements," he explains, "which are not admitted by the concurrent testimony of both parties."

The present-day reader will be struck not only by Gladstone's vivid depiction of the "Border Ruffians" and the correspondent's night in a Kansas City barroom, but also by other frontier scenes which he witnessed. Everywhere he found whisky-drinking, pistol-sporting, card-playing frontiersmen. Crudity, danger, and discomfort were normal on the Far Western frontier. He ascends the Missouri River by steamboat, crammed with adventurers, who rush to the bar and mix threats of violence against "Yankee Blue-bellies" with offers of hospitality, "Step up this way, old hoss, and liquor." Sleep was fitful for the correspondent, punctuated as it was with blasphemy from the bar, quarrels from the gaming table, two outbreaks of fire "at a tender point on the steamboat," and five or six groundings on sandbanks—all in one night.

The Western way of life is further limned in his vignette of Leavenworth. Here the rude life of the frontier and the bustle of capitalism coexist. The streets impede traffic with their stumps, and westerners inhabit wooden shanties and log houses. But the quay is piled high with goods, wagons wait in line as they prepare to cross the prairie, the hotel can offer only a chance of a place on the floor, and speculators bid up the prices of town lots. Gladstone's attention to urban life is all the more valuable in view of the heavy emphasis historians have traditionally placed upon the rural frontier.

His visit to a company of Sioux warriors left upon his mind "an impression of the profoundest melancholy." Taken captive for murder, they were solemn and impassive. Yet they received him hospitably, lit the calumet of peace, and revealed their humanity. His description of the Sioux's appearance is particularly striking; and the unfolding of their intense family feeling made him contrast the civilization of the savages with that of the lawless whites.

Besides such views of border life in the mid-
nineteenth century, the perceptive traveler tells us
what he saw of the Kansas conflict. Gladstone was
in the territory during the summer of greatest
excitement. The federal government's presence was
evidenced by Fort Leavenworth with its "white
walls and familiar flag staff." But its kindly commander, Colonel Sumner, was hampered by the
inertness of President Pierce. Gladstone traveled up
the Missouri River with "Governor" Robinson, a
prisoner of the proslavery element, target of repeated threats of frontier vengeance.

The correspondent's stay in Leavenworth over-
lapped the sitting of the Congressional investigating
committee, uncovering frauds amidst intimidation
of witnesses and a manifesto from "Captain Hemp."
The reporter intersperses his observations with a
history of the territory and another of the slavery
conflict in Congress. He seeks to explain to English
readers why law and order do not prevail in Kansas
and how the federal government has borne a large
share of the blame.

Finally, he returns to his impressions of the
spring of 1856. Civil war on the prairie commenced.
"The attack and burning of Lawrence," he tells

us "wrought a great change in popular feeling."
Simultaneously came news from Washington that
antislavery senator Charles Sumner had brutally
been beaten by a Southern congressman. "I well
remember the effect this had upon many, who concluded that the rule of force and violence had been
inaugurated." Proslavery marauders were now met
by antislavery guerillas. "As long as I remained in
the Territory, outrages and bloodshed were of daily,
frequently much more than daily occurrence."

After Gladstone departed, Kansas was pacified
by a new governor in time to help elect the Democrat James Buchanan president. However, the Kansas issue continued to divide the nation, as the
Supreme Court handed down its disastrous decision
in the case of Dred Scott, Lincoln and Douglas
debated the question of slavery in the territories,
and Congress wrestled with the notorious proslavery
Lecompton constitution. Kansans ultimately were
allowed to decide in favor of a free state, but by
that time the new Republican party had been
molded into a powerful sectional force, Southern
radicals were contemplating secession from a Union
they feared to be now unsafe for Negro slavery, and
the Democratic party had been split by the feud

between Buchanan and Douglas over Lecompton.

The reader must be warned that though Gladstone claims to have taken nearly all his testimony from proslavery men, he passed the judgment, "Among all the scenes of violence that I witnessed, it is remarkable that the offending parties were invariably on the proslavery side." Modern scholarship emphasizes that the riotous traits Gladstone depicted of the "Border Ruffians" were typical of frontiersmen and not confined to proslavery men. It points out that Governor Reeder, famed for his resistance to the "bogus legislature," had seriously compromised himself by his land speculations, and thereby gave President Pierce cause to dismiss him. It underscores the enormity of John Brown's atrocious murder of five proslavery men. It marks the fact that the antislavery men were, in the main, anti-Negro as well, not wanting the Black American, whether slave or free, in their midst. And it affirms the importance of the emotionalism which the antebellum generation labored under in trying to repress the impending conflict, an emotionalism which the foreign correspondent could not fully escape.

If historical research has revised some of Gladstone's impressions of Kansas, he in turn anticipated some researchers and offers valuable material for modern interpretation. Writing in late 1856, he foresaw what the future held for the territory's population—the preponderance of Northern settlers and the probability of the creation of a free state. Analysis of the 1860 census by W. O. Lynch confirms his expectations.

The discerning correspondent also realized that much of the conflict in Kansas had nothing to do with slavery. Settlers were concerned about land for themselves, not liberty for Negro slaves. They entered a claim by squatting, often only to be challenged by a belligerent claim-jumper. Squatters organized against jumpers, neighbors joining in, "guided by their political sentiments as to the side they shall espouse." Gladstone concluded, "More than one of the chief movements in the political history of Kansas have had their origin in difficulties arising from this prolific source." A close study of conflicts over Kansas land policy by Paul W. Gates elaborates this thesis.

His inspection of Eastern Kansas, river and prairie—much of it virgin land—is valuable. One must bear in mind he did not visit the Great Plains; and his description of its geography is derived, as he tells us, from the narratives of Colonel Frémont and others. In our day when the questions of race and law and order are to the fore, Gladstone's reports of Negrophobia and violence are pertinent.

The introduction by Frederick Law Olmsted, himself a traveler through the South, affords a contemporary American view of a house dividing. Olmsted's supplement continues the narrative of events about Kansas into early 1857.

The Englishman in Kansas went through English, American, and German editions in the 1850s. Today it is a rare book, almost impossible to come by in the second-hand book market, and if found it is offered at a prohibitive price. Yet historians have long recognized its value as a first-hand source. Albert Bushnell Hart reprinted an extract from it in his *American History Told by Contemporaries*, noting that it "is perhaps the most impartial contemporary narrative that we have." Herman Von Holst, James Ford Rhodes, Samuel Eliot Morison, and Allan Nevins each drew on Gladstone for their histories of the 1850s. A staple of Western and Civil War history, the narrative richly deserves to be made available to a new generation of readers.

JAMES A. RAWLEY

University of Nebraska

AMERICAN EDITOR'S

INTRODUCTION.

Having been requested to edit and introduce an American edition of this English book, I have thought I could best serve a public purpose by examining and setting forth its value and purport as evidence and intelligent European commentary upon the present exciting questions of our politics.

Mr. Gladstone, a kinsman of the distinguished ex-chancellor of the Exchequer of England, visited Kansas, at a moment of interest in its history, and in the history of our country. His opportunities of obtaining trustworthy information were good, and he appears to have used them calmly and diligently. As a foreigner, with claims of friendship, or even acquaintance, upon no one in the territory, except Colonel Sumner, who, as the military representative of the federal authority, was respected by both parties, he occupied a neutral position in their warfare.

Going back of these circumstances, I find that Mr. Gladstone arrived in New York near the beginning of the year 1856, with the ordinary motives of an English traveler of his class. From all I can learn of those who knew him here, his testimony on any subject should be received with particular respect. He is thought to observe closely and accurately, to study carefully, and to be slow in expressing the conclusions of his judgment. He is not known to have had, at this time, more knowledge of, or interest in, American politics, than is common among English conservative gentlemen—about as much, that is to say, as is common among us with regard to the affairs of Sweden or Brazil.

He proceeded, very soon after his arrival, to Washington, and thence further south, and, during the winter, enjoyed the hospitality of South Carolina and Mississippi. In the spring he continued his journey through Missouri, and so, finally, to Kansas, arriving at Leavenworth city on the 21st of May.

Our whole country was then hotly engaged in the presidential canvass. So great was the tumult in Kansas, and such was the temptation upon our editors and newsmongers to disallow or exaggerate the conflicting reports of its condition, according as their influence was likely to be favorable, or otherwise, to the success of one or another candidate, that it became, and has continued to be, very difficult for a cautious mind, not possessing private means of information, to form a confident judgment, first, as to the reality or extent of the alleged calamity of Kansas, and second, as to the absolute or relative culpability of either of the contending parties.

Readers, who have been accustomed to hear the "disturbances" in Kansas spoken of only as such as are "incidental to all new settlements," will, perhaps, be inclined to set down this calmly observant traveler as an impostor, or a romancer, when they find him describing the condition of the territory, upon his arrival, as

" a holiday of anarchy and bloodshed." Read-ers at the South, who have been accustomed to rely for contemporary history on Southern newspapers, or on those of the North in which information is given in a form adapted to the Southern market, may question if he were in his right mind when they find him testify-ing that: " among all the scenes of violence I witnessed, the offending parties were invariably on the pro-slavery side." Those who have seen nothing inconsistent with the official assurances of our late president, in the rapid humiliation of his three successively appointed governors, will hardly believe that the sympa-thies of an impartial, dispassionate, but justice-loving Englishman, could have been so immedi-ately engaged, on his arrival in the territory, for the Free-state party, as is implied by this narra-tive, unless his mind had been previously prejudiced against their opponents.

He had been in intercourse, almost from the moment of his landing in America, chiefly with Southern minds. He came to Kansas fresh charged from Southern social influence. And yet, before he had met a single avowed free-soiler in the territory, he evidently had a most painful impression of the injustice, tyranny, and persecution to which the majority of the actual settlers were subjected, and was well convinced that the pro-slavery party, and the influence of the South, acting through the federal government, was wholly to blame for this.

"But, surely," some indignant "democrat" will ask, "he would not have us suppose that the truth about Kansas has been monopolized all along by one party; that the black republican newspapers have been all right, and the rest all wrong?" This may have been the case without any advantage in veracity of character to those who told the truth. It may have happened that nothing could have served their purpose better than the truth. Certainly, if that purpose was to be served by proving a desperate determination on the part of the administration to establish slavery in Kansas, if necessary, at any cost of justice and humanity, and of our reputation with the world as a civilized people, nothing could have answered it better than what Mr. Gladstone, carefully studying the facts upon the ground, was led to consider the truth. He attributes the most honorable conduct, in all respects, as good citizens, to the Free-state party in the territory, while it would be difficult to describe a people more unfit to exercise the rightful privileges of citizenship than those whom he represents to be engaged, under the patronage of the federal authorities, in persecuting that party.

Such a contrast between the character of the emigrants from the Slave States and of those from the Free—both being, not many generations back, of the same origin and blood—would, indeed, be incredible, if there were not anterior reason to expect in the former a special proneness to violence, and a distrust, or habitual forgetfulness of law and civilized customs under exciting circumstances.

Such a dangerous quality — gravely dangerous, wherever this policy of so-called squatter sovereignty, involving, as it does, squatter warfare, shall be tried; and ten-fold grave to us of the North, since the recent decision of the Supreme Court,—such a dangerous quality is inbred and with every generation growing more

established in the character of the citizens of
the South.   It is so from the inexorable force
of circumstances—thus :

The title to property in slaves is derived
at no remote period, from certain vindictive
and lawless barbarians, who, having over-
powered an enemy, considered his life as
forfeited, and if they spared it, did so from
no regard to the abstract right or sacredness
of life, or any motive of humanity, but simply
for the purpose of enjoying the profits of his
labor.   His labor and abject submission to all
their demands upon him was the price of his
life, and with this understanding he was transferred to America.   At first the only persons
so held were "Black-a-moors," and all Black-
a-moors in the country were so held and considered, and only by terror of death, legalized and
insured by legislation and military force, continued to be held in the requisite habit of subordination for profitable labor, by their purchasers and
inheritors.   Hence, exceptional laws, exceptional
customs, and hence, irresistibly, a defection from
the usual sentiment of the sacredness of human
life, as far as the negro was concerned.   But as

the negro is, after all, really a human being, whatever affects him, inevitably affects all human beings associated with him. Thus arises a peculiar influence which must produce and reproduce peculiar qualities among people nurtured in a slaveholding community.

Hence, however our Southern fellow-citizens may continue to talk, and sentimentalize, and clothe themselves under ordinary circumstances in accordance with the customs, literature, laws and religious maxims of the rest of the civilized world, it is an inevitable effect of their peculiar institution to diminish in them that constitutional and instinctive regard for the sanctity of human life, the growth of which distinguishes every other really advancing people just in proportion to their progress in the scale of Christian civilization. Mr. Gladstone is not the first traveler whose studies among them have taught us this; nor is it necessary to assume the truth of his testimony to prove that there is this essential difference between the people of the Free and the Slave states. In what community, uninfluenced by slavery, could such a record be made, of recklessness unrestrained in regard to the life of its citizens, as the following, which is taken from the *Louisville Journal* (June, 1854), and was suggested by the "Mat Ward case," in which case, again, the alleged murderer was presently allowed to go free.

"There have been scores of notorious cases of murder and *acquittal* in this city. There was the case of Kunz who killed Schaffer. Kunz, hearing that Schaffer had spoken lightly of a member of his family, went to his coffee-house and cursed him. Schaffer picked up a small stick and went around the counter as if to strike Kunz, whereupon the latter thrust a deadly weapon into his breast and killed him. *He was tried and discharged without punishment.* There was the case of Delph who killed his uncle, Reuben Liter. Delph armed himself deliberately, and went to the upper market-house to meet Liter. He met him, sought a quarrel with him, and shot him dead on the spot. The quarrel was about a prostitute. *Delph was tried and acquitted by a jury.* There was the case of Croxton who killed Hawthorn. Hawthorn was in a coffee-house, sitting in a chair, drunk and asleep. Croxton struck him on the head in that condition with a brick-bat, and killed him. *He was acquitted by a jury.* There was the case of Peters who killed Baker. In Natchez, a long time before, Baker, in a fight, had wounded Peters, and made him a cripple. Peters being thus disabled, Baker supported him. The latter, after about a year, became very poor, and discontinued his bounty. Thereupon, Peters pursued him to this city, rode in the night in a hack to his house, sent the hackman to inform him that a gentleman and friend wished to see him on business, and when Baker came out and stood at the window of the hack, shot him dead instantly. *Peters was acquitted by the jury* and lived here for some years afterwards —long enough indeed to murder or try to murder a prostitute, upon whose bounty he subsisted. There was the case of the Pendegrasts, who killed Buchanan, a schoolmaster. The elder Pendegrast, with two of his sons and a negro, went to Buchanan's school-house with loaded guns and killed him, without giving him a chance for his life. *The jury gave a verdict of acquittal.* There was the case of Shelby who killed Horine in Lexington. The two dined at the same public table, and, upon Horine's going into the street, Shelby demanded of him why he had looked at him in such a manner at the table. Horine answered that he was not aware of having looked at him in any unusual manner. Shelby said — 'You did, and if you ever do it again, I will blow your brains out. I don't know who you are.' Horine responded — 'I know you, and suppose a man may *look* at you, if your name *is* Shelby.' At that, Shelby struck him with his fist, and without any return of the blow, and without any display of a weapon by Horine, for he was unarmed, Shelby shot him dead. Shelby was indicted, but *the jury found no verdict against him.* There was the case of Harry Daniel, of Mount Sterling, who killed Clifton Thompson. Daniel and Thompson were lawyers, and brothers-in-law. Thompson made some imputation upon Daniel in open court. Daniel drew a pistol and shot him dead in the presence of judge and jury. Thompson had a pistol in his pocket but did not draw it. *Daniel was acquitted by a jury.*"

Similar cases might be cited by the volume

in which public sentiment, finding its expression in the action of a jury, is proved to be constantly triumphant over all laws and ecclesiastical formulas in justifying homicide when it results from the quick and vehement anger of an undisciplined intellect. This is the natural consequence of the lurking danger everywhere present at the South, by which its citizens are compelled to hold themselves always in readiness to chastise, to strike down, to slay, upon what they shall individually judge to be sufficient provocation or exhibition of insubordination.

Southerners themselves may, perhaps, affirm that they are unconscious of this sense of insecurity, and this habit of preparation. But every habit breeds unconsciousness of its existence in the mind of the man whom it controls, and this is more true of habits which involve our safety than of any others. The weary sailor aloft, on the lookout, may fall asleep; not the less, in the lurch of the ship, will his hands clench the swaying cordage, but only the more firmly that they act in the method of instinct. A hard-hunted fugitive may nod in his saddle, but his knees will not unloose their hold upon his horse. Men who live in powder-mills are said to lose all conscious feeling of habitual insecurity; but visitors perceive that they have acquired softness of manner and of voice.

If a laborer on a plantation should contradict his master, it may often appear to be no more than a reasonable precaution for his master to kill him on the spot; for, when a slave has acquired such boldness, it may be evident that not merely is his value as property seriously diminished, but the attempt to make further use of him at all, as property, involves in danger the whole white community. "If I let this man live, and permit him the necessary degree of freedom, to be further useful to me, he will infect, with his audacity, all my negro property, which will be correspondingly more difficult to control, and correspondingly reduced in value. If he treats me with so little respect now, what have I to anticipate when he has found other equally independent spirits among the slaves? They will not alone make themselves free, but will avenge upon me, and my wife, and my daughters, and upon all our community, the injustice which they will think has been done them, and their women, and children." Thus would he reason, and shudder to think what might follow if he yielded to an impulse of mercy.

To suppose, however, that the master will pause while he thus weighs the danger exactly, and then deliberately act as, upon reflection, he considers the necessities of the case demand, is absurd. The mere circumstance of his doing so would nourish a hopeful spirit in the slave, and stimulate him to consider how he could best avoid all punishment.

But how is it in a similar case at the North? I have seen it. "I am sorry," says the farmer; "I am sorry you have such a bad temper, John. I can't afford to have you live with me, if you have not more respect for yourself and for me, than to play the blackguard. I will pay you what I owe you, and then we will part—part friends, if you please, for I bear no malice." And John goes, ashamed of himself, and with a sensible resolution to acquire a better self-government. The man who would knock John down, under these circumstances, especially if John were the weaker man, or taken at disadvantage, from behind, or with a weapon, would live without the respect, the confidence, or the affection of his neighbors. He would be called a vindictive, irritable, miserable old fool.

Mark the difference at the South. The same man would be called, and, perhaps, rightly, a brave, generous, high-toned, and chivalric gentleman. And, perhaps rightly, I say, for the impulses which would lead him, in the instant, and without reflection, to act decisively, that is, perhaps, to kill, and, at all events, to very cruelly hurt his fellow-being, and that without the smallest regard to fairness, it is not impossible might have been based on a generous sense of his duty to the public, and a superiority to merely selfish considerations. Thus slavery educates gentlemen in habits which, at the North, belong only to bullies and ruffians.

But, " planters sleep unguarded, and with their bedroom doors open." So, as it was boasted, did the Emperor at Biarritz, last summer, and with greater bravery, because the assassin of Napoleon would be more sure, in dispatching him, that there would be no one left with a vital interest to secure punishment for such a deed; and because, if he failed, Napoleon dare never employ such exemplary punishment for his enemies as would the planters for theirs. The emperors of the South are the whole free society of the South, and it is a society of mutual insurance. Against a slave who has the disposition to become an assassin, you find his emperor has a body-guard, which, for general effectiveness, is to the Cent garde as your right hand is to your right hand's glove.

It is but a few months since, in Georgia, or Alabama, a man treated another precisely as Mr. Brooks treated Mr. Sumner—coming up behind, with the fury of a madman, and felling him with a bludgeon; killing him by the first blow, however, and then discharging vengeance by repeated strokes upon his senseless body.* The

---

* "There are tender souls," says Mr. Elliott, in the "New England History," "who feel that after death the good alone live, and should only be spoken of, and this, in a degree, is true;" but "it is safest, it is most manly, to see men fairly, as they are, whoever they are, alive or dead." The late Mr. Brooks' character should be honestly considered, now that personal enmity toward him is impossible. That he was

man thus pitifully abused had been the master of the other, a remarkably confiding and merciful master, it was said—too much so ; " it never does to be too slack with niggers." By such indiscretion he brought his death upon him. But did his assassin escape? He was roasted, at a slow fire, on the spot of the murder, in

courteous, accomplished, warm-hearted, and hot-blooded, dear as a friend, and fearful as an enemy, may be believed by all ; but, in the South, his name is yet never mentioned without the term gallant or courageous, spirited or noble, is also attached to it, and we are obliged to ask, why insist on this? The truth is, we include a habit of mind in these terms which slavery has rendered, in a great degree, obsolete in the South. The man who has been accustomed, from childhood, to see men beaten when they have no chance to defend themselves ; to hear men accused, reproved, and vituperated, who dare not open their lips in self-defense, or reply ; the man who is accustomed to see other men whip women without interference, remonstrance, or any expression of indignation, must have a certain quality, which is an essential part of personal honor with us, greatly blunted, if not entirely destroyed. The same quality, which we detest in the assassination of an enemy, is essentially constant in all slavery. It is found in effecting one's will with another man by taking unfair advantage of him. Accustomed to this in every hour of their lives, Southerners do not feel magnanimity and the " fair-play" impulse to be a necessary part of the quality of " spirit," courage, and nobleness. By spirit they apparently mean only passionate vindictiveness of character, and by gallantry mere intrepidity.

the presence of many thousand slaves, driven
to the ground from all the adjoining counties,
and when, at length, his life went out, the fire
was intensified until his body was in ashes,
which were scattered to the winds and trampled under foot. Then "magistrates and cler-
gymen" addressed appropriate warnings to the
assembled subjects. It was no indiscretion to
leave doors open again, that night.

Will any traveler say that he has seen no
signs of discontent, or insecurity, or apprehension, or precaution; that the South has appeared
quieter and less excited, even on the subject
of slavery, than the North; that the negroes
seem happy and contented, and the citizens
more tranquilly engaged in the pursuit of
their business and pleasure? Has that traveler
been in Naples? Precisely the same remarks
apply to the appearances of things there at this
moment. The massacre of Hayti opened in
a ball-room. Mr. Cobden judged there was not
the smallest reason in the French king's surrounding himself with soldiers the day before
the hidden virus of insubordination broke out
and cast him forth from his kingdom. The

moment of greatest apparent security to tyrants is always the moment of their greatest peril. It is true, however, that the tranquillity of the South is the tranquillity of Hungary and of Poland ; the tranquillity of hopelessness on the part of the subject race. But, in the most favored regions, this broken spirit of despair is as carefully preserved by the citizens, and with as confident and unhesitating an application of force, when necessary to teach humility, as it is by the army of the Czar, or the omnipresent police of the Kaiser. In Richmond, and Charleston, and New Orleans, the citizens are as careless and gay as in Boston or London, and their servants a thousand times as childlike and cordial, to all appearance, in their relations with them, as our servants are with us. But go to the bottom of this security and dependence, and you come to police machinery, such as you never find in towns under free government : citadels, sentries, passports, grapeshotted cannon, and daily public whippings of the subjects for accidental infractions of police ceremonies. I happened myself to see more direct expression of tyranny in a single day and night at Charleston, than at Naples in a week; and I found that more than half the inhabitants of this town were subject to arrest, imprisonment, and barbarous punishment, if found in the streets without a passport after the evening " gun-fire." Similar precautions and similar customs may be discovered in every large town in the South.

Nor is it so much better, as is generally imagined, in the rural districts. Ordinarily there is no show of government any more than at the North : the slaves go about with as much apparent freedom as convicts in a dock-yard. There is, however, nearly everywhere, always prepared to act, if not always in service, an armed force, with a military organization, which is invested with more arbitrary and cruel power than any police in Europe. Yet the security of the whites is in a much less degree contingent on the action of the patrols than upon the constant habitual and instinctive surveillance and authority of all white people over all black. I have seen a gentleman, with no commission or special authority, oblige negroes to show their passports, simply because he did not recognize them as belonging to any of his neighbors. I have seen a girl, twelve years old, in a district where, in ten miles, the slave population was fifty to one of the free, stop an old man on the public road, demand to know where he was going, and by what authority, order him to face about and return to his plantation; and enforce her command with turbulent anger, when he hesitated, by threatening that she would have him well whipped if he did not instantly obey. The man quailed like a spaniel, and she instantly resumed the manner of a lovely child with me, no more apprehending that she had acted unbecomingly than that her character had been influenced by the slave's submission to her caprice of supremacy; no more conscious that she had increased the security of her life by strengthening the habit of the slave to the master race, than is the sleeping seaman that he tightens his clutch of the rigging as the ship meets each new billow.

The whole South is, in fact, a people divided against itself, of which one faction has conquered, and has to maintain its supremacy.

The "state of siege" is permanent. Any
symptoms of rebellion on one side, or of treachery on the other, cannot safely be left to the
slow process of civil law; every white man is
expected to deal summarily with them, and in
such a manner as to pervade with terror, cowardice, and hopelessness all the possibly disaf-
fected; and in many districts, where the conta-
gion of a bold or hot brain would be most
dangerous, the life of the whole white population is that of a "vigilance committee," every
man and woman grim-faced for a possible fero-
cious duty.

There is no part of the South in which the
people are more free from the direct action of
slavery upon the character, or where they have
less to apprehend from rebellion, than Eastern
Tennessee. Yet, after the burning of a negro
near Knoxville, a few years ago, the deed was
justified as necessary for the maintenance of order among the slaves, by the editor of a newspaper (the *Register*), which, owing to its peculiarly
conservative character, I have heard stigma-
tized as " an abolition print." " It was," he observed, " a means of absolute, necessary self-

defense, which could not be secured by an ordinary resort to the laws. Two executions on the gallows have occurred in this county within a year or two past, and the example has been unavailing. Four executions by hanging have taken place, heretofore in Jefferson, of slaves guilty of similar offenses, and it has produced no radical terror or example for the others designing the same crimes, and hence any example less horrible and terrifying would have availed nothing here."

The other local paper (the *Whig*), upon the same occasion, used the following language:

" We have to say, in defense of the act, that it was not perpetrated by an excited multitude, but by one thousand citizens—good citizens at that—who were cool, calm, and deliberate."

And the editor, who is not ashamed to call himself " a minister of Christ," presently adds, after explaining the enormity of the offense with which the victim was charged—" We unhesitatingly affirm that the punishment was unequal to the crime. Had we been there we should have taken a part, and even suggested the pinching of pieces out of him with red-hot pincers—the cutting off of a limb at a time, and then burning them all in a heap. The possibility of his escaping from jail forbids the idea of awaiting the tardy movements of the law."

How much more horrible than the deed are these apologies for it. They make it manifest that it was not accidental in its character, but a phenomenon of general and fundamental significance. They explain the paralytic effect upon the popular conscience of the great calamity of the South. They indicate that it is a necessity of these people to return in their habits of thought to the dark ages of mankind. For who, from the outside, can fail to see that the real reason why men, in the middle of the nineteenth century, and in the centre of the United States, are publicly burned at the stake, is one much less heathenish, less disgraceful to the citizens than that given by the more zealous and extemporaneous of their journalistic exponents—the desire to torture the sinner proportionately to the measure of his sin. Doubtless, this reverend gentleman expresses the uppermost feeling of the ruling mind of his community. But would a similar provocation have developed a similar and equally tumultuous, avenging spirit in any other nominally Christian or civilized people ? Certainly not. All over Europe, in every free-state — California, for significant reasons, temporarily excepted—in similar cases, justice deliberately takes its course ; the accused is systematically assisted in defending or excusing himself. If the law demands his life, the infliction of unnecessary suffering, and the education of the people in violence and feelings of revenge, is studiously avoided. Go back to the foundation of the custom which thus neutralizes Christianity, among the people of the South, which carries them backward blindly against the tide of civilization, and what do we find it to be ? The editor who still retains moral health enough to be suspected, as men more enlightened than their neighbors usually are, of heterodoxy, answers for us. To follow the usual customs of civilization elsewhere would not be safe. To indulge in feelings of humanity would not be safe. To be faithful to the precepts of Christ would not be safe. To act in a spirit of

cruel, inconsiderate, illegal, violent, and piti-
less vengeance, must be permitted, must be
countenanced, must be defended by the most
conservative, as a " means of absolute, necessary self-defense." To educate the people
practically otherwise would be suicidal. Hence
no free press, no free pulpit, nor free politics,
can be permitted in the South, nor in Kansas,
while the South reigns. Hence every white
stripling in the South may carry a dirk-knife in
his pocket, and play with a revolver before he
has learned to swim. " Self-preservation is the
first law of nature."

I happened to pass through Eastern Tennessee shortly after this tragedy, and conversed
with a man who was engaged in it—a mild,
common-sense native of the country. He told
me that there was no evidence against the negro
but his own confession. I suggested that he
might have been crazy. "What if he was?"
he asked, with a sudden asperity.

What if he was? To be sure; what if he
was? In fact, he was not burned because he
deserved it; nor, if we consider, because he
was believed by his rulers to have committed

the offenses charged upon him. It was not a question of evidence, of morality, but of expediency—simply, of self-preservation. His life depended not upon a conviction of his guilt, in the minds of his judges, but upon the opinion which the subject people of the county were likely to have about it, the same necessity requiring this jury of his peers to be degraded, cunning, and suspicious. To make them sure that their rulers are a strong and hard-hearted race, quick, sure, and terrible in their vengeance, was the object. It was a question no more of justice than of mercy, to the victim used in accomplishing the object.

Is it incredible that men, nurtured in communities whose most conservative and respectable classes, whose very professional teachers feel themselves justified in taking part in such barbarity, upon such grounds, should have been found, by Mr. Gladstone, guilty of purely barbarous conduct towards a people whose patient and self-controlling habits were so new to them that they could only ascribe them to a slave-like cowardice? Evidently, to the invaders of Kansas, it must have seemed a merciful treatment of those they had been taught to consider their enemies, when they fell into their hands, merely to hang, or shoot, and scalp them, without torture.

"No people," it has been said, "are ever found to be better than their laws, though many have been known to be worse." If, in the following advertisement, which was recently published in North Carolina, the proper-names and technical phrases were suitably changed, and it were presented to us by a traveler as coming from the Sandwich Islands, would it not strike us that it had been rather premature to class the natives of those islands among the Christian nations of the world?

"STATE OF NORTH CAROLINA, JONES COUNTY.—*Whereas*, complaint upon oath hath this day been made to us, Adonijah McDaniel and John N. Hyman, two of the Justices of the Peace of said county, by Franklin B. Harrison, of said county, planter, that a certain male slave belonging to him, named Sam, hath absented himself from his master's services, and is lurking about said county, committing acts of felony and other misdeeds. These are, therefore, in the name of State, to command the said slave forthwith to surrender himself and return home to his master; and we do hereby require the Sheriff of said County of Jones to make diligent search and pursuit after the said slave, and him having found, to apprehend and secure, so that he may be conveyed to his said master, or otherwise discharged as the law directs; and the said Sheriff is hereby authorized and empowered to raise and take with him such power of his county as he shall think fit for apprehending the said slave ; and we do hereby, by virtue of the Act of Assembly, in such case provided, intimate and declare that if the said slave, named Sam, doth not surrender himself and return home immediately after the publication of these presents, that *any person may kill and destroy the said slave, by such means as he or they may think fit, without accusation or impeachment of any crime or offense for so doing, and without incurring any penalty and forfeiture thereby.*

" Given under our hands and seals the 29th day of September, A. D., 1856.

"A. McDANIEL, J. P. : SEAL. :

"J. N. HYMAN, J. P." : SEAL. :

"$100 REWARD.

" I will give Fifty Dollars for the apprehension and delivery of the said boy to me, or lodge him in any jail in the State, so that I get him, or ONE HUNDRED DOLLARS FOR HIS HEAD.

"F. B. HARRISON."

May not the most conservative of us soon be obliged to consider less what we can do and suffer to retain the fellowship, than what we can do to guard against the sinister influences upon our own politics and society, of contiguous States, under the laws of which there is still the liability of such an exposition of constitutional barbarism? What is to be expected of such seed but such bitter fruit as that of Kansas, under the heat of Squatter Sovereignty?

The supreme judicial authority of the same State has declared that it would be preposterous, while the intention of holding the slaves in their present subjection was maintained, to consider it a crime for a white man to shoot a woman attempting to escape from the ordinary chastisement of indocility. It was decided (in the case of the State *vs.* Mann), by Justice Ruffin, "essential to the value of slaves, as property, to the security of the master, and to the public tranquillity," that such recklessness with human life should be unrestrained by the law.*

Let the reader who thinks there must be "two sides" to this story of Kansas, and that Mr. Gladstone has chosen to give his country-

---

* " Such service as is required of a slave, can only be expected of one who has no will of his own ; who surrenders his will in implicit obedience to that of another. Such obedience is the consequence only of uncontrolled authority over the body ; there is nothing else which can operate to produce that effect. The power of the master must be absolute to render the obedience of the slave perfect."—2. Devereaux's *N. C. Rep.*, 263.

men but one of them, remember that the necessity which has made the South thus exceptional among civilized States, in its law, must have made the people of the South much more exceptional among civilized mankind in their habits and character. Mr. Gladstone demonstrates but one consequence—that one which, being defended and apologized for by the President of the United States, has most injured the reputation of democratic institutions throughout the world. The world should recognize the fact that the disgraceful condition of Kansas, the atrocious system, which the federal government of the United States has been forced to countenance in Kansas, is the legitimate fruit of despotism, not of free government.

There are, however, many other characteristics of the people of the South which have had their origin in this necessity, which we of the North—since the absence of slavery is likely hereafter to depend on a local ordinance, since slavery is officially intimated to be national, and all opposition to slavery declared to be "sectional"—cannot afford to overlook. Would to God we had "nothing to do with it." But, as a Southern-born man said to me, lately, "It is a white man's question." Shall we hereafter exercise our rights as citizens of the United States, which are simply our natural rights as men, only by favor of Sharp's rifles and in entrenched villages?

It is, for instance, the foundation of that peculiar political coöperativeness and efficiency which we see in the people of the South. Nothing is safe if the slaves rise. Towards any party or measures, therefore, which, however indirectly, militate in the least against the everlasting subordination of the slave race, they act, as they do towards the slaves themselves, with the self-preserving instinct of a community always prepared for the attacks of a savage enemy. Hence, the intensity and completeness with which they give themselves up to any political purpose in which an increase of wealth, and, consequently, of stability in power, is involved for the slaveholding body. They engage in it as in war, and hold ordinary rules of morality and social comity to be suspended till they have gained their ends.

Their orators are wont to boast that they

belong to a military people.   What are termed the military qualities of the South are, again, the natural effects of this inherited watchfulness and readiness to meet, instantly and decisively, with cruelty and bloodshed, the first symptoms of insubordinate disposition on the part of their slaves.   These military qualities are, in fact, not such as are most valued for modern armies — individual staunchness, patience, and endurance of character, contributing to combined concentrativeness, precision, and mobility—but rather those of the feudal ages, or of savage warriors, the chief being mere belligerent excitability, readiness of resort to arms, an idolatrous estimate of the virtue of physical courage, and an insane propensity of that kind which leads Indian braves to amuse or disgust their visitors, as the case may be, by "scalp-dances" and monotonous recitative of their glorious achievements, past and prospective.   A government of force is ordinarily a government of threats and gasconading ostentation.   The subject must continually know that the master is confident in his strength.

We are well instructed by Humboldt, that the

only worthy purpose of the student of history
is to learn the influence which different circumstances have had on the development of character in mankind.   Doubtless, slavery has not
wholly failed of good effects upon the character
of our fellow-citizens of the South.   I do not
now inquire what those effects are, because
such an inquiry is not pertinent to the subject
of this book.   In the conduct of those who
represent the influence of slavery in Kansas,
only the worst qualities which it is possible for
men to acquire have hitherto been displayed.
Even the measurable success with which they
have, to this moment, maintained their conquest,
is due to no good judgment, energy, or bravery
of their own, but is evidently entirely dependent
on what, to such observers as Mr. Gladstone,
must be the most incredible and inexplicable
circumstance -in the whole sad business—the
encouragement they receive in their villainy
from the democratic party of the Free-states, and
the constant countenance, supplies, reinforcements, and patronage of the federal administration.   Withdraw this; let the oppressed citizens
generally feel that it would be right, and proper,

and lawful to deal with their present rulers as they have been dealt with by them, and the savages would disappear from the land as the more manly Indians have before them, and then the present scandal of Kansas would be lost in the natural peace, order, and prosperity of a society, no member of which need have aught to fear but from his own folly, nor aught to hope but from his own industry, as surely as the fire-blackness of its winter prairies is submerged in the green flood of its spring.

Is it unpatriotic to thus show the incompatibility of slavery with good citizenship?

The people of the South are "my people." I am attached to them equally as to those of Massachusetts or Pennsylvania. My blood and my fortune are equally at their service. I desire their prosperity as I do that of no other people in the world. I look upon slavery as an entailed misfortune which, with the best disposition, it might require centuries to wholly dispose of. I would have extreme charity for the political expedients to which it tempts a resort.

But it seems to me now, that such inexcusable scoundrelism in our common matters, as has been shown in Kansas, should make us consider if charity has not been carried too far; if the forbearing, and apologetic, and patronizing disposition towards everything in the South, or of the South, or for the South, is not as much calculated to bring us into difficulty as the reckless and denunciatory spirit attributed to the abolitionists. Have not thousands of our Northern people so habituated themselves to defend the South that they have become as blind to the essential evils and dangers of despotism as if they were themselves directly subject to its influence?

In the South itself, there has been for many years a school of fanatics, who maintain that slavery is essential to a high form of civilization; who, in their selfish anxiety to maintain it, have trained themselves to think that its influence is wholly ennobling and refining, christianizing and civilizing. These views are so flattering to the predominant bad propensities developed by slavery that they are propagated with a zeal and a success like that of the immediate followers of Mahomet. The

characteristic vices of the middle ages are
unearthed and enshrined under the name of
chivalry, and the youth of our country is
taught to reverence a reckless, blundering,
and blood-thirsty buccaneer as a "second
Washington," and a silly, romantic, swaggering
poltroon, who can talk wickedly of women and
wear a graceful feather, as "the Marion of
Kansas."

Against this gospel no one dare contend with
a spirit and boldness at all comparable to that
of its apostles. Books, periodicals, and newspapers, are interdicted, if they maintain the faith
which was universal among its friends in the
South when our Union was formed. However
calm and respectful their manner, they are denied
the service of the United States mails ; those who
receive them are denounced as abolition traitors ; gentlemen who acknowledge themselves
to privately hold similar opinions, and who are
on terms of friendship with their authors, feel
obliged to "discountenance" them. "If I
should express my real opinions," said one,
himself a large slaveholder, "it is not unlikely
I should be mobbed and my life placed in

jeopardy by men who never have owned and never will own a single negro."

Nay, have we not recently seen that, for a mere act of customary politeness to a political opponent, and of respect to a high official of our national government, Mr. Aiken, of South Carolina, the wealthiest citizen and the largest slave-owner of that state, has been denounced and insulted, as guilty of a "gross wrong" to his constituents? There is no "democratic paper" in all the South, believes the editor of the South Carolina *Times*, that has not condemned the act; no paper which has approved of it. In all the South, not one editor still lives to sympathize with the instincts of a gentleman of the old school. So complete is the success of the new gospel of slavery in its own country.*

---

* The argument with which the South Carolina *Times*, in the article referred to, disposes of the claim of courtesy, strikingly sustains the opinions I have expressed, that it is to an habitual precaution against insubordination of the slaves that we are chiefly to attribute the peculiar customs and manners of the South. Speaker Banks is an opponent of the extension of slavery—not an abolitionist in the political sense; "but," says the *Times*, "we regard him as beyond

At the North, we have not only " public
documents" sent us by the ton, but many self-
styled democratic newspapers, which follow,
as near as can be thought discreet for propa-
gandists, in the same course—denying the evils
of slavery, apologizing for them, or, with as-
tounding impudence, in the case of these Kansas
barbarisms, charging them upon the persecuted
and long-suffering victims, whom, also, they
hold up to scorn, as " traitors" and " abolitionists." The most successful journal in the
service of the administration here in New
York, is not satisfied thus negatively to serve
the purposes of the slavery fanatics, but takes
the aggressive against freedom, daily arguing
" the universal failure of free society," earn-
estly combating " the wide-spread delusion
that Southern institutions are an evil, and

---

the pale of a refined courtesy—excluded by his own acts.
If incurable fanaticism be a merit, Speaker Banks has it.
If inexpiable treason be a virtue, Speaker Banks can claim
it. To prove this we need only repeat what we have said
before. Mr. Speaker Banks avows sentiments that lead
directly, and lead inevitably, to insurrection, rapine, and
murder! He boldly proclaims himself an enemy to the
South—to the institutions of the South."

their extension dangerous," and diligently advocating the claims to universal adoption of a system, living under the influence of which Jefferson declared the citizen "must be a prodigy who retained his morals and manners undepraved;" which Patrick Henry testified to be "at variance with the purity of our religion;" which Mason held "to produce the most pernicious effects on manners," and calculated to draw "the judgment of heaven upon a country;" which Franklin termed "an atrocious debasement of our nature," and "a plan for the abolition" of which Washington declared to be "among his first wishes."

When the Supreme Court finds slavery to have been considered a national institution by these statesmen in the construction of our constitution; when this opinion, at variance with every impression we have received from our fathers, is welcomed with cheers and congratulations in the North, as by the State Democratic Convention of Connecticut; when nearly all the newspapers of the South, and one quarter of those at the North, express nothing but satisfaction with the criminality of the

late administration in Kansas; nothing but
charity or admiration for the savages nurtured by
slavery to fight its battles; nothing but sneers
and maledictions for the grand results of free
government manifested in the patient, orderly,
and industrious character of their victims;
when with the ruling, though minor party, of
our citizens, freedom and the " Rights of man"
are subjects only of ridicule—slavery only of
apology or laudation; when foreigners find
border-warfare the most interesting subject of
observation on our continent; when the subjects of every crowned head in Europe are
pointed to Kansas for a caution against dreams
of self-government; when our army is used as a
reserve force for bands of robbers, while they
murder the sons, and ravish the daughters, and
devastate the property of our dearest friends
and neighbors, and all in the service of slavery,
is it not reasonable to believe that there is
greater danger of our forgetting the evils which
the people of the South suffer from slavery
than of our overlooking the advantages which
they claim to enjoy from it?

PREFACE.

THE following pages comprise the chief substance of a series of letters on the condition of
Kansas which appeared during the past winter
in the columns of *The Times* newspaper. By
the kind permission of the Editor, the material
then used has been introduced into the present
volume, in which a more complete and detailed
portraiture is attempted of those scenes of
peace and war which came under the author's
observation whilst travelling in the western
territories of America in the early summer of
1856.

To enable the reader better to comprehend
the political strife of which Kansas has been
the arena, the author has introduced into this
volume a few concluding chapters, which comprise in brief outline the principal events

which have marked the history of this contest. The author has not attempted argument upon the political questions involved. He has carefully avoided the subject of Slavery, except where he speaks incidentally of the economics of free and slave labour. He has not made himself the advocate of the measures adopted by the Free-state party to form a State Government, although the Committee of Investigation appointed by Congress report in favour of the Constitution thus adopted, as one which embodies the will of a majority of the people. His simple desire has been to present facts, and he cheerfully leaves it to others to draw such inferences as they may deem legitimate.

As it has been the author's object to restrict his statements to that which he has seen or been able personally to verify whilst in the territory, it necessarily follows that the events which have occured since his visit are more cursorily noticed. He has only introduced these later events in order to give completeness to the narrative; but, as his information has been gathered solely from those of whose trustworthiness he has had full proof in connection with the events with which he is personally familiar, the author feels confidence in the accuracy of the statements which the few closing pages contain.

To the two interesting volumes which have recently appeared in America upon the subject of Kansas, by Mr. William Phillips and Mrs. Robinson, the author is especially indebted for facts contained in the concluding chapters of this Book. Had they reached his hands before his own volume was in the press, they might have been further serviceable to him. As it is, they have aided him in writing of that which has occurred since his visit, whilst they give valuable confirmation to the statements contained in the narrative of his own investigations.

Lastly, the author hopes it will not give pain to any one of his many valued friends in America, that he should have addressed himself to a subject which they cannot but grieve over as he does. He can assure such, that he has had no object in view but to hasten the application of a remedy to that which is a sore evil. Had similar events taken place in his own country, he would have felt warranted in speaking of them with far greater severity. If any feel yet aggrieved, he can only repeat the maxim :—

"Amicus Socrates, amicus Plato, sed magis amicus veritas."

But of those whose friendship is a prize worth treasuring—and many such the author rejoices to number in America—he feels assured it will never be said that their friendship was conditional on silence as to the truth. The author commits his Book, therefore, to his true friends and to all others, known or unknown, in the belief that the truth, spoken without animosity and with a sincere desire to render beneficial service, will, whilst it contributes towards this end, be misapprehended or misjudged by none.

KANSAS.

CHAPTER I.

Excitement in relation to Kansas.—Difference of Opinion.—The President's Special Message.—Washington.—Contest as to a Seat in Congress.—Rival Legislatures.—Appointment of a Committee of Investigation.—Southern Meetings.—Volunteers in arms.—Missouri.—Powder and Shot.—Advertisements.—A Crisis at Hand.—Visit to Kansas.

WHEN in New York, during the latter part of the winter of 1855–6, I heard daily discussions on the condition of affairs in the far western territory of Kansas. Some of the newspapers had their special correspondence at what was termed "the seat of war," and all were eager to supply the latest intelligence from the scene of contest. At Washington, whilst the house of Representatives was busy choosing a Speaker,—a process which lasted through nine weeks, and required one hundred and thirty-three ballots,—the President, without waiting for the organization of the house, made Kansas the subject of a special message. Yet, while all parties agreed in recognizing the existence of disorder in Kansas, there were strange differences in the light in which that disorder was regarded.

Many of the public journals spoke with indignant censure of bloodshed and forcible invasion from neighbouring states, as well as of violent interference with the people of Kansas in the exercise of their rights of suffrage. The President spoke in mild terms of "disturbing circumstances," "irregularities," and "inauspicious events," adding, that "whatever irregularities might have occurred in the elections, it seemed too late now to raise that question."

The papers spoke of a legislative body claiming authority over the residents of Kansas, which they had not elected, but which had been forciby thrust upon them with pistol and bludgeon by a lawless horde from the State of Missouri. The President said, that "for all present purposes the legislative body, thus constituted and elected, was the legitimate assembly of the territory."

The people of Kansas were represented by a large portion of the press as groaning under a most oppressive legislation, and as craving deliverance from a fraudulent legislature, and from tyrannical laws enacted by that legislature. The President made it the conclusion of his message, that he felt it his imperative duty to exert the whole power of the federal executive for the vindication of these laws, for the suppression of all resistance to them, and for the support thereby of public order in the territory. He begged all good citizens to help him thus to restore peace, and asked for an appropriation to defray the expense of enforcing the laws, and thus maintaining public order in Kansas.

The difference was apparent. A large portion of the people denied the legality of the legislative power in the territory, and bitterly complained of the injustice with which that power was exercised, and the oppressions under which they were consequently placed. The President said it was too late now to raise the question of legality,—they must submit; that if they did submit, peace would ensue ; but, if otherwise, the federal force and the army of the United States would be employed against them to compel their submission.

At Washington I gained further insight into the question.

I saw the tall figure of General Whitfield moving about the House of Representatives, and heard lengthened arguments whether he or the ex-govenor Reeder was the rightful delegate of Kansas. These discussions ended in permission being given to Mr. Whitfield, the pro-slavery delegate, to occupy a seat in the house without voting, the question of right between him and Mr. Reeder being reserved.

Every day I heard Kansas and its contest argued upon in the Senate Chamber and in the House of Representatives, in the bustling hall of the National Hotel, and in private political circles. I heard that which I conceived to be the extreme on the one side and on the other, and was not long in discovering that, while the President and the advocates of Southern views maintained the authority of the illegally constituted Territorial Legislature of Kansas, and of the judiciary and other officers appointed by it, the opposite party, with a large portion of the people of Kansas themselves, asserted the claims of an incipient State Legislature, which they had elected in the prospect of its being admitted as a state.

A double legislature, a double judiciary, a double set of civil appointments throughout each claiming sole prerogative, the State Legislature calling the Territorial a fraud, and the Territorial calling the State Legislature a sham ; such a political condition appeared strangely anomalous.

On the one side of the question a very long report from the Committee of Territories was presented to the Senate by Mr. Douglas, and on the other side, a "minority report," from the same committee by Mr. Collamer. At length, on the 19th of March, Congress gave a temporary check to the protracted discussion by accepting a motion which sprang from the Committee on Elections, to the effect that a committee should be appointed to investigate and collect evidence in regard to the troubles in Kansas generally, and particularly in regard to any fraudulent or violent proceedings that might have accompanied the elections in the territory.   No member from any one of the Southern states voted in favour of the investi-

gation, but happily a majority was given by
the Northern states, and the Committee on
Inquiry was appointed. This resolution was
passed whilst I was in Washington, and I made
up my mind at the same time, if practicable,
in the spring of the year, to carry out an
investigation on my own account, and to satisfy myself, if possible, as to where the truth
lay, which seemed buried beneath so overwhelming a mass of contradictory assertions.

Later, when in South Carolina and other
Southern states, I witnessed extraordinary
meetings, presided over by men of influence,
at which addresses of almost incredible violence were delivered on the necessity of " forc-
ing slavery into Kansas," of " spreading the
beneficent influence of Southern institutions
over the new territories," and of " driving
back at the point of the bayonet the nigger-
stealing scum poured down by Northern fanaticism."

These meetings generally terminated by an
urgent appeal for men and money. The result
of this public agitation was, that large compa-

nies were formed of young men who were enthusiastic for slavery, and subscriptions of large amount were made to send these, who were already at blood-heat with excitement, armed into the territory, and furnished with means of support during the continuance of the campaign.

In the latter part of May I found myself in the State of Missouri. For two or three months I had read none but Southern journals, I had spoken with none but Southern men, I had heard none but Southern views, and, as a consequence, I was fully furnished with the South-side aspect of the controversy.

The accounts from Kansas indicated a most threatening condition of affairs. Party bitterness had apparently increased. Law existed only for party purposes, and deeds of violence were of almost daily occurrence.

The St. Louis papers contained advertisements, by the half-column, of rifles, revolvers, gunpowder, and lead. One of these advertisements may serve as an example of the whole. I extract the following from the *Daily Missouri*

Republican, published at St. Louis.   Attention is arrested by the heading, "KANSAS," in large type, and the representation of a revolver in the margin.

KANSAS.

 JUST RECEIVED, by *Adams & Co's. Express*, a large and fine Assortment of DOUBLE and SINGLE

SHOT-GUNS,

which will be sold cheap for Cash.

We have also on hand an Assortment of our own Manufacture of

RIFLES,

so well known for the past thirty years throughout the Western country.

Emigrants to Kansas should not fail to call at ————— —————, and examine our Stock before purchasing elsewhere.

————— —————.

The Committee of Inquiry appointed by Congress I understood to be at the time in Kansas, carrying on their investigations. Through the kindness of friends, I had been furnished with letters to Colonel Sumner, who was in command of the United States troops, and other persons of influence in the territory. Being already in the adjoining State, and events of great moment in the history of Kansas, if not the breaking out of civil war itself, being evidently at hand, I felt disinclined to forego my purposed visit.   Five hundred more miles of river navigation would take me to the scene of conflict.   I resolved to go and see for myself.

CHAPTER II.

Outburst of Violence.—Burning of Lawrence.—Contents of
the following Chapters.—Political Parties.—Dramatis Per-
sonæ.—Federal Appointees.—Border-ruffian Ring-leaders.—
Leaders of the Free-state Cause.

COULD I have made choice of a period in which
to visit Kansas, which should be most rife with
incident and best adapted for the successful
prosecution of my inquiries, I could not have
selected one more favourable than that of my
actual visit. The affairs in the territory had
reached a crisis. At that moment unresisted
oppression had reached its highest point, and
the severest blow was struck which Kansas has
yet received. Greater individual suffering may
have been inflicted later, but May 21st, 1856,
was a day which turned the tide of popular
feeling, and thus terminated one era in the history of the Kansas struggle, and introduced
another.

On that eventful day the town of Lawrence,

without offence or crime, was attacked by armed forces, some six or eight hundred strong; its principal hotel, the largest private building in the territory, was battered down and then reduced to ashes; the printing-offices of the Free-state journals were set fire to, the editors having been previously captured and carried off as prisoners; the type and presses were destroyed and cast into the Kaw river; and the city itself was given over to a merciless sack. On the same day, and by the same agency, occurred the firing of Governor Robinson's house on Mount Oread, after it had been made throughout the day the head-quarters of the invading troops. Governor Robinson himself had been arrested a few days before while travelling eastward, and was a prisoner during the attack upon Lawrence, as well as for four months subsequent. His arrest was made without a legal warrant, and his tedious confinement in the gaol at Lecompton was equally without sentence or trial.

But the blow aimed at the Free-state cause in the destruction of Lawrence, and the seizure and imprisonment of some of its most active adherents, brought a severe recoil. A spirit of resistance was evoked, public feeling throughout the country was aroused, and it is not improbable that this great temporary triumph of the pro-slavery party in Kansas may prove itself in the end its most signal defeat.

In the following chapter I purpose describing, as accurately as possible, from information gained on the spot, the events of the siege of Lawrence. It may be right to add that, whatever testimony I gathered in Kansas was, for the most part, obtained from pro-slavery men. My account, therefore, is rather the result of the admissions of these than of the assertions made by Free-soil advocates. I have endeavoured to omit all statements which are not admitted by the concurrent testimony of both parties.

In a succeeding chapter I will give some detail of events witnessed by myself, which will illustrate the earlier portion of Governor Robinson's captivity and the spirit of his captors, during a short period when it was my fortune to be his companion in travel.

As an introduction to these narratives, however, it may be of service to many readers to have presented in a single view the names of the principal personages who have borne their part, whether nobly or ignobly, in the earlier stages of Kansas history. A more particular delineation of some of the most noted of these characters may be attempted later, when occasion requires. But the following list will interpret for the reader the names most frequently occurring in the narrative, and will indicate the official capacity or political views possessed by the individuals themselves.

Of political parties in Kansas, the two main divisions are, of course, the Free-state and the pro-slavery parties; but the latter exhibits a further distinction, according as its adherents are moderate and constitutional in their maintenance of Southern views, or endeavour to force their principles upon the territory by powder and shot. The latter policy is known as "border-ruffianism."

COLONEL E. V. SUMNER.—Colonel of the 1st regiment of cavalry, and, until the latter part of 1856, commander of the United States troops in Kansas. Colonel Sumner won distinction in the Mexican war, and has had much experience of military affairs in the Western territories.

ANDREW H. REEDER.—The first Governor of Kansas appointed by the President. A man of erect form and determined aspect, hair slightly gray, more apt to listen than to commit himself by speech. He received his appointment as a friend of the Southern interest, but offended his party by failing to espouse the border-ruffian cause. He was removed from the governorship by the President in the summer of 1855, and was subsequently elected by the Free-state people as delegate to Congress, in opposition to Whitfield.

DANIEL WOODSON.—The Secretary of the territory during Reeder's governorship, and afterwards acting Governor until the appointment of Shannon. He is a tall, somewhat handsome young man; comes from Arkansas, and is true to the South, but did not join in all particulars the extreme party.

WILSON SHANNON.—The second Governor of

Kansas appointed by the President. An extreme Southern man in politics, of the border-ruffian type. Under Shannon's governorship, all the worst deeds that have marked the history of Kansas have taken place. As the head of the executive in the territory during the border-ruffian rule, Governor Shannon's name will need to be mentioned only too frequently.

J. W. WHITFIELD.—The delegate returned chiefly by Missourian votes, to represent Kansas in Congress. "General" Whitfield, as he is commonly called, is a resident of Missouri, and was formerly an Indian agent. He is a tall man, of uninviting expression of countenance and somewhat sinister aspect. Latterly the General took the field, and became very active in the border-ruffian campaign.

SAMUEL DEXTER LECOMPTE.—The Chief Justice of Kansas territory, appointed by the President. A small, fair-complexioned, keen-eyed lawyer, Judge Lecompte has rendered himself infamous as the type of judicial border-ruffianism, even as Shannon represents the same

principle in the executive. The town of Lecompton has been named in honour of the
Judge, and has been designated by the territorial legislature as the capitol of the territory.

J. B. DONALDSON.—The Marshal of the territory, also appointed by federal authority. Like
Shannon, a native of Ohio, and, like him, also
determined to serve the power which placed
him in office. He is a man somewhat advanced
in life, but has made himself remarkable, even
amongst his associates, for his unscrupulous surrender of his powers as United States Marshal
into the hands of the border-ruffian leaders.

W. P. FAIN.—Deputy U. S. Marshal. A
Georgian, and a despicable follower of Donaldson in his measures of extermination.

SAMUEL J. JONES.—Formerly Postmaster in
the town of Westport, Missouri; afterwards
made Sheriff of Douglas County in Kansas,
and chief agent in the execution of the be-
hests of the border-ruffian judiciary. A remarkably mean and contemptible man, but

one who has had much power placed in his hands.

DAVID R. ATCHISON, of Platte County, Missouri, formerly Senator for the State, President of the Senate, and Vice-President of the United States; known on the border as "General Atchison," or "Old Dave," Captain of the Platte County Rifles, and a prime leader among the border-ruffians. A thorough Missourian in his language and habits, as well as in his political views. To General Atchison and the four or five whose names follow, belongs the credit of having commenced and been the chief agents in sustaining the border-ruffian policy in Kansas.

J. H. STRINGFELLOW, living in the town of Atchison, K. T. A doctor; editor of the *Squatter Sovereign*, a violent border-ruffian paper; member of the House of Representatives in the Territorial Legislature, and chosen to the Speakership of the same. Called generally Dr. Stringfellow. His editorial articles breathe out threatenings and slaughter continually.

BENJAMIN FRANKLIN STRINGFELLOW. — A brother of the former, practising as a lawyer, in partnership with Peter T. Abell, in Weston, Missouri. Called by distinction " General" Stringfellow. A border-ruffian to the core. Rather over the middle age, fair in complexion, but furious in his crusade against freedom.

WILLIAM P. RICHARDSON.—Another of the Missourian brotherhood, who has been engaged in the plot from the commencement. He was elected to the Teritorial Legislature as Member of Council, and, on the organization of the militia by the legislature, was made Major-General of the Kansas Teritorial Militia.

DR. GEORGE W. BAYLESS, COL. BROWN, COL. YOUNG, COL. BOONE, all residents of Missouri, and leaders in the cause of slavery extension.

REV. THOMAS JOHNSON.—Superintendent of the Shawnee Manual Labor School and Mission ; appointed by the United States Government to teach the Shawnee Indians farming, letters, and the principles of Christianity. It will be well for the Indians that they should not follow his practice. He is a warm adherent of border-ruffianism. As President of the Council, he has been elevated to the highest office in the Territorial Legislature, and some absurd attempts were once made to make him Governor.

COLONEL BUFORD, of Alabama, and COLONEL TITUS, of Florida; two zealous Southern men, who came with other officers into Kansas about April, 1856, at the head of large companies of volunteers from the Southern States, to aid the border-ruffian cause.

CHARLES ROBINSON.—A native of Massachusetts, by profession a physician, and who has had some experience of life in California. Although under forty years of age, his cool self-possession, caution, and soundness of judgment marked him out as the leader of the Free-state cause. When the Free-state party formed a military organization, Dr. Robinson became Major-General and Commander-in-Chief; and, on their forming a civil power, he was elected Governor under their State constitution.

COLONEL JAMES H. LANE.—A young man, full of impetuosity and fiery daring ; obtained his rank as Colonel in the Mexican war ; has also sat in Congress. He has devoted himself with great spirit to the Free-state cause in Kansas, was made Brigadier-General in the Free-state army, and was chosen as President of the Constitutional Convention which met at Topeka.

SAMUEL C. POMEROY.—Also a Free-state General, and one who has taken, from the first, an active interest in the settlement of Kansas.

WILLIAM Y. ROBERTS.—Made Lieutenant-Governor under the Free-state constitution. A man who likes, apparently, to see himself in office, but lacks the nerve for high occasions.

CHAPTER III.

Situation of Lawrence.—Eventful History.—The Winter Campaign of 1855.—Earthwork Fortifications.—Organized Defence.—Determination to "wipe out Lawrence."—The Southern War-cry.—Peaceful Policy of Free-state Inhabitants.—Reinforcement of the Border-ruffian Army.—Sheriff Jones's reported Assassination.—Sheriff Jones's Tours of Arrest.—Hotel and Newspaper offices to be abated as Nuisances.—May 21st.—Position of the besieging Army.—The War-flag raised.—Arrests of Citizens.—Surrender of Arms demanded by Jones.—Entry of the Forces.—General Atchison's Address to his men.—Demolition of Printing-offices.—Cannon.—Burning of Free-state Hotel.—Flight of the Women and Children.—General Pillage.—Firing of Governor Robinson's House.—Southern Hearts filled with Joy and Pride.—"Law and Order" triumphant.

SOME forty miles up the Kaw or Kansas river, and some forty miles, therefore, from the Missouri state-line, stands the town of Lawrence. It is situated at a very beautiful spot on the right bank of the river. Behind the town, on the southwest, at the distance of nearly a mile, rises a hill of considerable elevation, known as Mount Oread. Towards the east, undulating prairie-land stretches for many miles, intersected by the Wakarusa Creek. And at a spot where the prairie, at the foot of a somewhat high bluff, slopes towards the woody margin of the Kaw, stands the busy little town itself, now so famous in Kansas annals.

The autumn of 1854 witnessed the erection of the first log-huts of Lawrence by a few families of New England settlers. During the year 1855 its population increased rapidly, chiefly by the arrival of emigrants from the Northern States. Its log-hut existence gave way to a more advanced stage, in which buildings of brick and stone were introduced; and the growing prosperity of the " Yankee town" early began to excite the jealousy of the abettors of slavery. Viewed as the stronghold of the Free-state party, it was made the point of attack during what was called " the Wakarusa war" in the winter of 1855. Before the termination of this its first siege, the necessity of some means of defence being manifest, the inhabitants of Lawrence proceeded to fortify their town by the erection of four or five circular earthworks, thrown up about seven feet in height, and measuring a hundred feet in diameter. These were connected with long lines of earthwork entrenchments, rifle-pits, and other means of fortification. Whilst these engineering operations were being carried on, the men might have been seen, day and night, working in the trenches, in haste to complete the defence of their Western Sebastopol. The inhabitants were also placed under arms, formed into companies, with their respective commanders, under the generalship of Robinson and Lane, had their daily drill, mounted guard day and night upon the forts, and sent out at night a horse-patrol to watch the outer posts, and give warning of approaching danger.

The pacification which followed the Wakarusa campaign in December, 1855, afforded only a temporary lull. Although war had ceased, the people did not cease to carry arms, and used them, when occasion offered, with fatal effect. The Missourians did not conceal that they were organizing another invasion, which should effectually "wipe out Lawrence," and win Kansas for slavery, " though they should wade

to the knees in blood to obtain it." The
Southern states were being appealed to far and
wide, to aid by men and money in the extirpa-
tion of every Northern settler. The spirit of
the pro-slavery party may be gathered from
their journals, from the columns of which extracts like the following might be made in any
number. After speaking of Free-state men as
being " willing to violate the constitution of
their country, which explicitly recognizes
slavery," the *Kickapoo Pioneer* (Dec. 26) pro-
ceeds :

" Should such men receive any compassion
from an orderly, union-loving people ? No !
It is this class of men that have congregated at
Lawrence, and it is this class of men that Kansas must get rid of. And we know of no better
method, than for every man who loves his
country and the laws by which he is governed,
to meet in Kansas and kill off this God-forsaken
class of humanity as soon as they place their
feet upon our soil."

Again, in an extra number of the same journal, published Jan. 18, 1856 :

" Forbearance has now ceased to be a virtue ;

therefore we call upon every pro-slavery man
in the land to rally to the rescue. Kansas must
be immediately rescued from the tyrannical dogs.
* * * * Pro-slavery men, law and order men,
strike for your altars! strike for your firesides!
strike for your rights! sound the bugle of war
over the length and breadth of the land, and
leave not an abolitionist in the territory to re-
late their treacherous and contaminating deeds.
Strike your piercing rifle-balls and your glitter-
ing steel to their black and poisonous hearts!
Let the war-cry never cease in Kansas again,
until our territory is wrested of the last vestige
of abolitionism."

Surrounded by so much fire and fury, which
was not confined to mere words, the non-resistance of the Free-state people was remarkable.
Lawrence kept itself fortified, continued its
drills, had its " Committee of Public Safety,"
and did not return the shots frequently fired
against it by passers-by at night. In the mean
time the Free-state delegates met at Topeka,
organized the State Legislature, made application to the federal power for the admission of
Kansas into the Union with a free constitution,
and petitioned the President, although vainly,

for protection from wrong. Their steadfast adherence to these peaceful measures, and their remarkable moderation in the midst of much that might have excited a spirit of resistance, was doubtless due chiefly to the peaceable policy ever counselled by their Commander-in-Chief and Governor, Charles Robinson, whose wise caution preserved the Free-state party from doing a single act which might serve their adversaries as a reasonable excuse for an appeal to arms.

The month of May arrived, and the state of parties continued as before. The pro-slavery, or, as it was commonly termed, the border-ruffian army, had, however, gained strength by large reinforcements from the States. Colonel Buford was there with his determined bands from Alabama, Colonel Titus from Florida, Colonel Wilkes and others with companies from South Carolina and Georgia, all of whom had sworn to fight the battles of the South in Kansas. The President, too, through his Secretary-at-War, had placed the federal troops at the command of Governor Shannon, and the Chief Justice Lecompte had declared, in a notable charge to a grand jury, that all who resisted the laws made by the fraudulently elected Legislature were to be found guilty of high treason.

In the mean time the people of Lawrence, some fifteen hundred, probably, in number, silently awaited the coming blow.

The chief aim of the party in power was to find an excuse for an attack upon Lawrence. The inhabitants of the town, and especially their " Committee of Public Safety," were as resolute in not giving any such occasion. At length the report went through the country, that Samuel Jones, the Sheriff of Douglas County, who had been most active in making arrests of Free-state men, with a view to excite provocation, was shot—shot in the spine— basely assassinated by blood-thirsty abolitionists. His murder must be avenged, they said, though at the sacrifice of every abolitionist in the territory. Yet Jones was not murdered. He had been slightly wounded by a ball, from whose pistol none could say ; but how little the Free-state party was chargeable with the act may be judged from the indignation meeting held on account of it in Lawrence on the following day, the resolutions they passed condemnatory of the act, the reward they offered for the apprehension of the guilty person, and the care they took of Jones himself, lodging him in their own Free-state Hotel, and attending to his wants until he was able to go forth and persecute them anew, with a more deadly rage than ever.

That Sheriff Jones had been assassinated, that Governor Reeder had resisted a deputy marshal in an attempt to arrest him, that the people of Lawrence were turning the Free-state Hotel into a fortress, with parapets and port-holes for the use of cannon and small arms, that there were mines beneath the streets of Lawrence, to be sprung in case of attack— these were the stories current in every one's mouth when I first approached the territory, and out of which abundant capital was made, in order to inflame the people against Lawrence.

Meanwhile, Sheriff Jones rode about the country with a "posse" of United States troops, arresting whomsoever he pleased; the

grand jury declared the Free-state Hotel and
the offices of the *Herald of Freedom* and *Kansas
Free-State* newspapers in Lawrence to be nuisances, and as such to be removed; Governor
Robinson and several other men of influence in
the Free-state cause were severally seized and
held as prisoners; Free-state men were daily
molested in the highway, some robbed, and
others killed; and a constantly increasing army
was encamping right and left of Lawrence,
pressing daily more closely around it, and
openly declaring that their intention was to
"wipe out the traitorous city, and not to leave
an abolitionist alive in the territory."

The policy pursued by the inhabitants of
Lawrence during these events was a very
pacific one. They resolved, through their
Committee of Public Safety, to offer no manner of resistance to the acts, however unjust,
of those possessed of authority, and even ten-
dered their services to the Marshal, to aid him
in serving his processes on those whom he desired to arrest. They also made representations
of the danger of their position to the federal
and territorial authorities, but without effect.

At length the day approached when **Law-rence** was to fall. On the night previous to May 21st, could any one have taken a survey of the country around, he would have seen the old encampment at Franklin, four miles to the southeast of Lawrence, which was occupied during the Wakarusa war, again bristling with the arms of Colonel Buford's companies, brought from the States. This formed the lower division of the invading army. On the west of Lawrence, at twelve miles distance, he would have seen another encampment in the neighbourhood of Lecompton, occupied by the forces under Colonel Titus and Colonel Wilkes. These were reinforced by General Atchison, with his Platte County Rifles and two pieces of artillery; by Captain Dunn, heading the Kickapoo Rangers; by the Doni-phan Tigers, and another company under Gene-ral Clark, as well as by General Stringfellow, with his brother, the doctor, who had left for a time his editorship to take a military command, and other leaders, who brought up āll the law-less rabble of the border-towns, to aid in the attack. These on the west of Lawrence formed the upper division. A large proportion were cavalry. The general control of the troops was in the hands of the United States Marshal, Donaldson, the whole body, of some six or eight hundred armed men, being regarded as a *posse comitatus* to aid this officer in the execution of his duties.

By three o'clock on the morning of the 21st, Colonel Titus, with about two hundred horsemen, appeared on the crown of Mount Oread, overlooking the town of Lawrence. In a few hours the remaining portion of the upper division had reached the same position. Some occupied Governor Robinson's house, situated on the declivity of the hill towards the town, which they made their headquarters; others planted their cannon, of which they had several pieces, on the brow of the hill, in a position which commanded the city. Shortly after, the besieging army was reinforced by the arrival of the lower division, under Colonel Buford. A blood-red flag, inscribed with the words "Southern Rights" on the one side, and "South Carolina" rudely painted on the other, was then raised over the invading troops.

During the forenoon Fain, the Deputy-Marshal, entered Lawrence with some assistants, to make arrests of its citizens. He failed, however, in provoking the resistance desired, on which to found a pretext for attacking the city; for the citizens permitted the arrests to be made, and responded to his demand for a "posse" to aid him. He dined at the Free-state Hotel, at Messrs. Eldridge's, the proprietors', expense, and returned with his posse and his prisoners to the hill occupied by the troops.

The United States Marshal had now, he stated, no more need of the troops; but, as Sheriff Jones had some processes to serve in Lawrence, he would hand them over to him as a *posse comitatus*.

Accordingly, in the afternoon, Jones rode into Lawrence at the head of twenty or more men, mounted and armed, and placed himself in front of the Free-state Hotel, demanding of General Pomeroy the surrender of all arms. He gave him five minutes for his decision, failing which the *posse* would be ordered to bombard the town. General Pomeroy gave up their brass howitzer and some small pieces, the only arms that were not private property. Jones then demanded the removal of the furniture from the hotel, stating that the District Court for Douglas County had adjudged the hotel and the two free-state newspaper offices to be nuisances, and as nuisances to be removed, and that he was there as Sheriff to execute these indictments, and summarily remove the obnoxious buildings.

In the mean time the forces had left the hill, and were at the entrance of the town, under Titus and Buford, Atchison and Stringfellow. General Atchison's address to his men on this occasion may be cited as an example of the mode of speech adopted by a late Vice-President of the United States. From various reports of it made at the time, the following is gathered, being in substance and language that in which all agree :—

" Boys, this day I am a Kickapoo ranger, by ——. This day we have entered Lawrence, 'Southern Rights' inscribed on our banners, and not one —— abolitionist has dared to fire a gun. No, by ——, not one! This, boys,

is the happiest day of my whole life. We have
entered the ———— city, and to-night the abolitionists will learn a Southern lesson that they
will remember to the day of their death. And
now, boys, we will go in with our highly honourable Jones, and test the strength of that
———— Free-state Hotel, and learn the Emigrant Aid Society that Kansas shall be ours.
Boys! ladies should be, and I trust will be,
respected by all gentlemen; but, by ——, when
a woman takes on herself the garb of a soldier
by carrying a Sharpe's rifle, then she is no longer
a woman, and, by ——, treat her for what you
find her, and trample her under foot as you
would a snake. By ——, come on, boys!
Now to your duties to yourselves and your
Southern friends! Your duty I know you will
do; and if a man or woman dare to stand before you, blow them to hell with a chunk of
cold lead!"

Thus inspirited by their leaders, the Sheriff's
posse, or rather the armed and inflamed rabble,
proceeded to their work of demolition. The
South Carolinians planted the red flag, with
its lone star and its inscription of "Southern
Rights," upon the roof of the large hotel.
The banner of the Doniphan Tigers bore the

device of a tiger rampant. Another flag had black and white stripes; and a fourth displayed in blue letters on a white ground the following admonitory lines :—

> " Let Yankees tremble,
>   And abolitionists fall !
> Our motto is,
>   ' Give Southern rights to all.' "

The newspaper offices were the first objects of attack. First that of the *Free State*, then that of the *Herald of Freedom*, underwent a thorough demolition. The presses were in each case broken to pieces, and the offending type carried away to the river. The papers and books were treated in like manner, until the soldiers became weary of carrying them to the Kaw, when they thrust them in piles into the street, and burnt, tore, or otherwise destroyed them.

From the printing offices they went to the hotel. The Eldridge House, or Free-state Hotel, was a building of size and strength. It was solidly built of stone and concrete, consisted of three stories above ground, had a breadth of five windows in the front, and

six windows on the side of the house. The
Messrs. Eldridge had just completed its furnishing, and had well filled its store-rooms and
cellars in anticipation of the wants of their
guests.

As orders were given to remove the furniture, the wild mob threw the articles out of
the windows, but shortly found more congenial
employment in emptying the cellars. By this
time four cannon had been brought opposite
the hotel, and, under Atchison's command,
they commenced to batter down the building.
In this, however, they failed. The General's
" Now, boys, let her rip !" was answered by
some of the shot missing the mark, although
the breadth of Massachusetts-street alone inter-
vened, and the remainder of some scores of
rounds leaving the walls of the hotel unharm-
ed. They then placed kegs of gunpowder in
the lower parts of the building, and attempted
to blow it up. The only result was, the shat-
tering of some of the windows and other limited damage. At length, to complete the work
which their own clumsiness or inebriety had
rendered difficult hitherto, orders were given to

fire the building in a number of places, and, as a consequence, it was soon encircled in a mass of flames. Before evening, all that remained of the Eldridge House was a portion of one wall standing erect, and for the rest a shapeless heap of ruins.

The firing of the cannon had been the signal for most of the women and children in Lawrence to leave the city. This they did, not knowing whither to turn their steps. The male portion of its citizens watched, without offering resistance, the destruction of the buildings named, and next had to see their own houses made the objects of unscrupulous plunder.

The sack of Lawrence occupied the remainder of the afternoon. Sheriff Jones, after gazing on the flames rising from the hotel, and saying that it was "the happiest day of his life," dismissed his "posse," and they immediately commenced their lawless pillage. In this officers and men all participated, and they did not terminate until they had rifled all the principal houses of whatever articles of value they could lay their hands upon, and had destroyed that which they could not carry away.

Finally, Governor Robinson's house on Mount
Oread was set fire to, after it had been searched
for papers and valuables, and its burning walls
lit up the evening sky as the army of despera-
does, now wild with plunder and excesses, and
maddened with drink, retired from the pillaged
city.

The value of the property stolen and destroyed during the day in Lawrence is estimated
to have amounted to nearly thirty thousand
pounds sterling.

Life was fortunately not taken, as the inhabitants of Lawrence disappointed their invaders
of a fight, by offering no resistance. The only
deaths which occurred were of two young men
in the pro-slavery ranks. One shot himself
accidentally through the shoulder; the other
was killed by the South Carolina flag sweeping
a brick from the roof of the hotel, which fell upon
the young man's head and caused his death.

Thus ended a day which filled Southern
hearts with joy and pride. The next day the
journals were filled with glowing accounts of
victory, and of the glorious triumph obtained
by law and order over fanaticism.

CHAPTER IV.

THE day following the attack upon Lawrence being that of my own arrival in the territory, I am able to supply its later history from personal observation, and will endeavour to illustrate the condition of Kansas at that excited time by a narrative of things seen and heard during the period of my visit.

The border-ruffian forces employed in the siege and sack of Lawrence being disbanded, were to be seen on the following day spreading over the roads towards the east, carrying fury and violence wherever they went. Having once been taught that robbery and outrage, if committed in the service of the South, were to be regarded as deeds of loyalty and obedience, these ministers of a self-styled " law and order" were slow to unlearn a doctrine so acceptable. The day, like the preceding, was extremely hot, the thermometer standing at above ninety degrees; their thirst knew no bounds; and when a barrel of Bourbon, or Monongahela, or Double Rectified was accessible, they forgot even in some instances to ask the politics of its possessor. Thus through the day they sustained their turbulent fury, and when night came, it found them prepared for any excesses.

It was on that night that I first came in contact with the Missourian patriots. I had just arrived in Kansas city, and shall never forget the appearance of the lawless mob that poured into the place, inflamed with drink, glutted with the indulgence of the vilest passions, displaying with loud boasts the "plunder" they had taken from the inhabitants, and thirsting for the opportunity of repeating the sack of Lawrence in some other offending place. Men, for the most part of large frame, with red flannel shirts and immense boots worn outside their trousers, their faces unwashed and unshaven, still reeking with the dust and smoke of Lawrence, wearing the most savage looks, and giving utterance to the most horrible imprecations and blasphemies; armed, moreover, to the teeth with rifles and revolvers, cutlasses and bowie-knives, — such were the men I saw around me. Some displayed a grotesque intermixture in their dress, having crossed their native red rough shirt with the satin vest or narrow dress-coat pillaged from the wardrobe of some Lawrence Yankee, or having girded themselves with the cords and tassels which the day before had ornamented the curtains of the Free-state Hotel. Looking around at these groups of drunken, bellowing, bloodthirsty demons, who crowded around the bar of the hotel, shouting for drink, or vented their furious noise on the levee without, I felt that all my former experiences of border men and Missourians bore faint comparison with the spectacle presented by this wretched crew, who appeared only the more terrifying from the darkness of the surrounding night. The hotel in Kansas city, where we were, was the next, they said, that should fall; the attack was being planned that night, and such, they declared, should be the end of every place which was built by Free-state men, or that harboured "those rascally abolitionists." Happily this threat was not fulfilled.

A number of these men became my companions for the night, as I went up by one of the Missouri steamboats from Kansas to Leavenworth city, which, as a convenient centre, I desired to make my headquarters whilst investigating the condition of affairs in the territory. The other fellow-passengers were, for the most part, of a like order. A few Germans, carrying their stock-in-trade, to turn an honest penny by peaceful traffic, while other people were fighting; a company of New Mexicans, making their way through Kansas to Santa Fé; three or four persons more gentlemanly in appearance, to whom I shall again have occasion to refer; and, for the rest, a crowd of adventurers little better than those just taken on board, who might be classed generally under the head of "border ruffians," made up, with a single exception or two, our travelling party for the night.

A general rush to the bar ensued. Already maddened with whisky, each would treat his fellow in arms : —

"Step up, and liquor here, you sir. A heap finer this stuff than that there rot-gut ashore. Here, you sir; don't be askeard. One of our boys, I reckon? All right on the goose, eh? No highfalutin' airs here, you know. Keep that for them Yankee Blue-bellies down East. If there's any of that sort here, I reckon they'd better make tracks, mighty quick, and that's a fact, while I'se on board, unless they want to make a quicker road out than they came in. Yes, sir, this yere tool of mine [handling a pistol], it isn't the first time it has seen a Blue-belly. If there's any of that 'ere sort aboard, I say they'd better clear out, that's sartin. We ain't agoin' to stand them coming here, we ain't. Isn't their own place down East big enough for them, I should like to know? We ain't agoin' to stand their comin' and dictatin' to us with their —— nigger-worshipping, we ain't. I reckon we'll make the place hot enough for them soon, that's a fact. Here, boys, drink. Liquors, captain, for the crowd. Step up this way, old hoss, and liquor."

And thus the midnight talk went on — talk which I neither care to remember nor to repeat, and in which I am compelled to omit the fearful expletives of blasphemy which interrupted, not every sentence merely, but every word or two of the dialogue. Others sat down to cards, and quarrelled over their losses; some, more sleepy, threw themselves upon the cabin floor to rest, for it was already two hours past midnight. In all, there were nearly two hundred on board; and as it was evident that the majority must sleep on the floor, I hastened to secure one of the berths, and thus to seek relief, if possible, from the distracting noise. In a smaller degree, I had had so much of a similar experience before, that I managed to sleep, only awakened at times by a louder shout from the bar or the gaming-table.

In the morning, like my fellow-travellers, I was early astir. My Western companions, accustomed to frequent potations, seemed already sobered down by their few hours' rest. If less boisterously demonstrative, however, in relation to " Yankee Abolitionists " than in the night, the change was only to an animosity of a more calculating and determined character. News of fresh strife had been received during the night. "Extras" of the different journals, in the form of printers' slips, containing the latest intelligence, were put on board and largely circulated. These invariably contained distorted accounts of the events of the hour, and appeals of a most inflammatory character. As they were read aloud to the eager listeners, they gave occasion to renewed determination to "fight the nigger-worshipping crew to the last drop of blood." One "extra" I obtained, issued by the *Border Times* at Westport, in which the outrages at Lawrence were announced beneath the heading, "THE KANSAS BALL OPENED— WAR IN EARNEST." In another, a Lecompton paper, the narrative was headed, "LAWRENCE TAKEN — GLORIOUS TRIUMPH OF THE LAW- AND-ORDER PARTY OVER FANATICISM IN KAN- SAS." When cold-blooded murder, which has left behind it destitution, widowhood, and orphanage, comes to be regarded by journalists as the mere opening of a ball and a ground for exultation, it is not to be wondered at that the men who perpetrated these deeds were eager to

acquire fresh glory in the achievement of fur
ther " triumphs."

A single incident must suffice as an illustration. Before I had left my berth many minutes,
I was attracted by the blustering talk of one
of my fellow-travellers—" one of the most respectable merchants in Weston," as I was
informed, but one who, as was evident, did not
deny himself in the rum-punch, gin-sling, whis-
ky-straights, brandy-cocktails, and other com-
pounds issued at the bar.

This respectable merchant was surrounded,
as he stood in the cabin of the boat, by a
circle, which I joined. Out of a side-pocket
protruded the head of a pistol ; in his hand
he brandished another, loaded, as he told us,
and ready for action. With threatening aspect
and attitude, he poured forth, amid many oaths,
the following language, addressed to us all :—

" I am bound to bring down some one before
I'm done ; I tell you, by —— I am. I'll teach
these infernal nigger-stealing Free-soilers a lesson right peartly, that's a fact. If there's a dog-
gauned Abolitionist aboard, I should like to see
him, *that* I should. I'm the man to put a chunk

o' lead into his woolly head, right off; yes, *sir*, that's what I'll do."

Then, looking round at each of us, "I reckon I can raise the top off the head of ere a one of you with this hyere tool. Speak the word, and, by ——, I'm your man. That's so. I should like to see the first Free-soiler that opens his mouth; that I should. I'd send him to hell pretty quick, afore he know'd what he was about; that's what I'd do. I'm a mighty ce-urious customer, *I* am."

And so thought, probably, one of his hearers, for he said to the curious customer, "Come, old hoss, won't you have some breakfast?" The old horse was not to be so easily diverted, however.

"Breakfast! think I'd be after breakfast when I've got my duty before me? No, *sir*, exercise is the thing for me—not eating. I tell you I'm bound to drop some one afore I'm done—*that* I am. I've got to fight for the liberties of my country and our glorious constitution, and rid the place of those cowardly blue-bellied Yankies. Yes, *sir*, that's what I've got to do. I should like to know what they've to do in this hyere place, with their snarlin', sneakin', whittlin'-o'-nothin' ways. I tell you

there's not a man amongst them as knows how
to fight. I should like to see the first one as 'll
open his mouth here,—that's what I should
like to see. I tell you I'm a ce-urious customer. Yes, sir-ree; my dog knows that,"
pointing to a large dog that seemed prepared
to stand by his master for better or worse.
Then, "I should like to sot my eyes on the
man as would touch that 'ere dog of mine. I'd
lay him dead in a moment, *that* I would. Just
see me."

None of us felt inclined to touch the dog, and
the respectable merchant returned to his politics and patriotism.

"No Northern nigger-stealers here. I'll fix
'em up mighty smart, I will. I ain't here for
nothing, and that you'll see, just about as soon
as anything. Yes, *sir*, I only want to see the
first Free-soiler here. I'll drop the first one of
you that opens his mouth for abolition cusses;
I be dog-gauned if I don't."

And thus this valiant patriot went on for
about half an hour, ringing the changes on these
few forms of expression, and giving every one
an opportunity to accept his challenge and take
the consequences.

I remained no longer in this Western merchant's immediate presence than was necessary to prevent my becoming an object of his suspicion. Being anxious to obtain some information as to the hotels or other places of resort in Leavenworth, I went up on the hurricane-deck, having been told I should there meet with some who could answer my inquiries. I found on the upper deck the few more gentlemanly persons to whom I have referred, but whom, until this moment, I had not seen. One or two appeared to be United States officers, men of education and refinement. Another, a gentleman more advanced in years, held himself somewhat apart, and appeared engaged in anxious thought. He had an eye full of bright intelligence, and wore the aspect of one who was superior to those about him. I gained the information I sought from one of the officers, and took his recommendation to go to M'Carty's hotel at Leavenworth, where he himself was about to stop. I did not know as yet, however, who were my companions, and could only get evasive replies to my inquiries on the subject from the clerk of the boat.

I again descended to the cabin. The respectable merchant from Weston was still continuing his challenges, pistol in hand.

" I should like to see the first one as 'll open his mouth. I reckon he'd have to take the change mighty smart. Lead's the best argument for these infernal white-livered Yankees. Let me alone for tamin' them down; yes, *sir;* let me alone for that, I say. I reckon they won't be a tryin' on this game again a little whiles. That's just about what *I* think."

And so on without intermission.

At my side stood a young man who had lived for some years in Kansas territory, trading with the Indians. We had travelled in company during four or five days in coming up the Missouri, and our intercourse had led to a certain degree of mutual confidence. He was a thorough Western man, and, at the same time, a favourable specimen of his class, possessing in a large degree the better traits which mark the Western character, and displaying few of the worse. As we should soon have to part, he inquired of me what part of the Union I came from. I replied, in a tone which I hoped would not catch the ear of the noisy patriot in arms, that he had mistaken me as a native of the Union, and that I belonged to the old country, my home being London.

"Indeed," said my friend the Indian trader, "I calculated you were a Northern man. Your dress and looks aren't like our people's out West."

"That is probable," I replied.

"Yes, that's so," he proceeded, "and there's several aboard as have been talking about you, and they've all set you down for a Northerner."

I hinted, in reply, that I had no desire to excite remark on board, and glanced suggestively at our neighbour who was threatening to blow the brains out of the first Northern man who should open his mouth. My friend perceived my meaning immediately, and, dropping his voice to a whisper, said :—

"Well, Colonel, just let me, as one that knows the ways of the people here, give you a word of caution, which you may find useful, now that you're setting foot in these here Western diggins. Don't let a soul of them know that you're an Englishman. Should it get out, it's just as much as your life is worth, mind that.   That's the state we're in just now, all alongside of that cursed slavery question. If you say you're an Englishman it's all the same as being a Yankee; not a bit better. And you know the law there—a Yankee is a nuisance, and nuisances must be abolished. That's what they all say there.   So you mind, Colonel ; and don't forget what I say."

I thanked my friendly adviser, and told him I had already determined to follow his counsel.

As for himself, he said, he did not believe the Southern men had any right to do what they had done in Kansas ; but being a thorough Western man, and known in the territory for years, he could go about and they would not touch him, especially as he did not take part with the Abolitionist fanatics.   If they did touch him, everybody knew what would be the consequence.   And as I looked at his fine athletic frame, and noticed the powerful muscle of his arm and the steady gaze of his eye, long trained to guide the bead of his rifle, I thought I, too, could perceive what would be the consequence of having this Western man for an enemy. But he had given me wise counsel and kind, and I was glad to think the son of the prairie was my friend.

CHAPTER V.

By about nine o'clock, A.M., the steamboat had
reached Leavenworth city. It would excite a
smile if I were to describe the aspect of this
" city" of log-houses and wooden shanties; as
it would if I were to narrate the manifold
adventures incident to Western travel. But
that is beside my purpose. The majority of
the passengers, with myself, landed. A great
crowd received us, all evidently eager with
expectation and excitement. To my astonish-
ment, the moment after landing I perceived

that the older gentleman whom I had seen on the hurricane-deck of the steamboat was a prisoner. Surrounded by a number of persons, including the United States officers, he was led off towards M'Carty's hotel, my purposed place of stay. "Who's that they've got there?" "Who's that been caught, eh?" were the eager questions put on many sides. "It's Governor Robinson, been brought round from Lawrence by way of Kansas city," was the reply of one in the crowd. "*Governor* Robinson, *Governor* Robinson! Who taught you to call that infernal nigger-stealer Governor, I should like to know?" was the instantaneous rejoinder. "Say the word again, and I will blow your brains out for an Abolition traitor; he is *Doctor* Robinson, and nothing else, that's what he is, and he shan't be that long. It's time we'd got shet of these dog-gauned Abolitionists." Thus surrounded by the menaces and imprecations of a savage mob, the Free-state Governor was led up the steep road which conducted to the small wooden house known as M'Carty's hotel.

I followed, and, first inquiring for my own accommodation, was met by the answer that if

I would come in again at night I might take a chance of a place on the floor. This was sufficiently unpromising. I then went to a larger house, the headquarters of the Pro-slavery party, but met with no better reception. Leaving, therefore, the question of accommodation, I returned to M'Carty's, where I was informed I could get a meal. Governor Robinson I found in the front room of the house; he was standing up, and was being put through a close examination by those in the room. A larger number had collected outside the open windows and door, and, as I stood amidst this crowd, I heard the constantly repeated expressions, "Let *us* get hold of him; —— if we don't sarve him out, powerful quick. The hangin' bone villain, he may say his prayers mighty smart now. I'll be dog-gauned if we don't string him up afore the day's out. Hangin's a 'nation sight too good for him, the mean cuss. He ought to have a shot through his head right away—that's how I'd sarve him."

Sick of hearing such expressions, mingled with the vilest oaths, I went into the office of the hotel, and sat down on a vacant chair to meditate and to observe. In the corner of the room, in place of trunks and travelling-bags, were rifles and double-barrels, dirks and sticks, of that weight and calibre which only a Western American thinks of carrying. The clerk and the persons passing in and out had nothing to speak of but "the fighting." On the counter were papers, heading their columns with the words—"War to the knife." Everything around was suggestive of warfare and blood-shed.

I had sat for a few minutes, when there entered a man—a Southerner by his very looks. "Hand me a pair out of them hundred pistols I left with you, Captain," were the words which, with a slow drawling voice, he addressed to the clerk at the counter. The large number of instruments owned by our visitor suggested that he was taking advantage of the existing demand, by "trafficking" a few small-arms. We awaited, however, his remarks. Glancing his cool eye at me and another in the room, and anticipating probably that we might desire an explanation, he slowly added—"I've just had a turn down here with a —— Free-soiler."

We still looked inquiringly, and as he adjusted his pistols in his belt, he proceeded for our satisfaction—"I'd got nothing with me. I didn't ought to have left these here tools behind this morning, I allow. Anyways, I didn't leave him till I made him give in. He came out with his onremittin' abolitionism. I settled him though, a heap quicker, I reckon, than he expected. I tell you how I done. I jest put my hand behind me, like this, the same as though I had got my pistols with me, and looked kinder ugly—down on him like, you know; and so, with my hand upon the pistols, as he reckoned, he didn't stand out long. But I felt mighty bad, I tell you, till I got the draw on him, as he expected. Still I wasn't goin' to stand his sarcy talk, in course, so I jest shut him up mighty quick." By this time the pistols were adjusted, and as he walked out, their valiant wearer continued a kind of soliloquy—"Well, reckon I'm fixed now! They won't be so sarcy with their talk now that I've these here fixins on. I brought him down a kinder smart, I reckon. Expect he felt chawed up some. Well, I calculate they won't be so sarcy now. I'll see jest who next I'll meet."

From the city of Leavenworth I went before noon to visit the Fort. I found it at about three miles' distance, beautifully situated on a lofty bluff, overlooking the Missouri, and sufficiently elevated in position for its white walls and familiar flag-staff to be seen for many miles across the far-stretching prairie. There was a feeling of security and retirement about the Fort, which rendered a resort to it an agreeable relief from the angry excitement which prevailed in all other places. Add to this, a visit to Fort Leavenworth gave one the opportunity of meeting the only society the neighbourhood afforded. I have many pleasing recollections of my intercourse on these occasions with the officers stationed at Fort Leavenworth, chief among whom must be mentioned Colonel Sumner, at that time in command of the garrison, with whom I had much interesting conversation on the troubled condition of the territory, and from whom I received, during my stay in Leavenworth, much kindness and hospitality.

The scenes of the twelve hours I have described—from midnight of the 23rd of May, 1856, to noon of the 24th—were repeated during my few days' stay in Leavenworth, without intermission. As the night advanced, the ceaseless whisky-drinking showed its fruits. Pistols went off sometimes unguardedly; knots of people collected at each street-corner. The bar-rooms in the hotels, which were all political clubs, became crowded with noisy debaters, planning the great deeds they were to perform on the morrow. Numberless gambling-houses were the resort of others. Cards could have been picked up in the streets by the score; and in a town where the very first demands of civilization were wanting in the furnishing of the house, there was no lack of such costly indulgences as gaming-tables, which reminded one of Baden-Baden or Hamburg. No element of vice or crime seemed to be absent. Every species of shameless wickedness and unchecked outrage met one's gaze at every turn.

My own accommodation at night was of the worst. I was subject to frequent interruptions of armed intruders, whom I could not keep out

of my room; and by day I had to listen perpetually to conversation which was painfully
revolting. On the day of my arrival, the
seizure of Governor Robinson was, of course,
the principal topic. He had been seized, I
ascertained, during the previous week, at Lexington, in Missouri, whilst openly travelling
towards St. Louis, in company with Mrs.
Robinson. His captors were not at the time
possessed of any indictment against him, but
detained him by main force, and threats of
murder at the hands of the crowd, if he should
fail to consent. He was then conveyed to
Westport, on the border line, and detained
there until the attack upon Lawrence was
completed. The following night he arrived
under guard at Franklin, within four miles of
Lawrence, where he was intercepted by a message from Governor Shannon, requiring him to
be taken to Leavenworth by way of Kansas
city, to avoid a rescue. By a circuitous route,
therefore, he was again brought down to Kansas
city, where he arrived in the night, a short
time before the departure of the steamboat on
board of which I first met him.

Throughout the day stories were circulated about the Free-state governor, for which there was not the shadow of a foundation. Every minute some fresh charge was brought, or some new threat uttered against him.

"If I had caught his track, —— if I wouldn't have shot him dead. I told him so at the inquiry. I'd have smashed his head right out. I don't care if it isn't true. I told him I should believe it, all the same, till he proved it wasn't. He is a flung up, pilfering, —— puppy; that's what he is, fix it which way you like."

Judge Lecompte came down to Leavenworth in the evening to see Dr. Robinson. The next day I also saw Governor Shannon. Rumours were put into circulation that the Free-state men intended to attempt a rescue of their leader during the night. Committees were held in consequence to organize a defence; and few probably retired to rest that night in Leavenworth city with the expectation of remaining till morning without a summons to arms.

The Committee of Investigation appointed by Congress was also sitting at Leavenworth during my stay. The enormities that were brought to light embittered exceedingly the Pro-slavery party; and many threats were made against the persons of those who gave their testimony, as well as the lives of the commissioners. Some of these threats, whilst they were terribly real, were at the same time sufficiently ludicrous; as, for example, the following manifesto, which appeared one Monday morning during my stay in Leavenworth, scrawled upon a piece of paper, which was affixed to the door of the office occupied by the Committee.

" *May*, 26.

" Messrs. Howard and Sherman.

" Sirs, with feelings of Surprise and Disgust wee have been noticeing the unjust manner in which you have been Conducting this Investigation. Wee wish to inform you can no longer sit in this place.

" Wee therefore request You to alter your Obnoxious course, in order to avoid the Consequences which may otherwise follow.

" Capt. Hemp—in behalf of the citizens.
" Leavenworth City—1856."

Mr. Howard, on entering the office, was observed to take down the paper containing the symbolical Capt. Hemp's declaration of intentions, and, folding it up with a smile, placed it in his pocket.

On the third day of my stay, several Free-state men were arrested; among them Judge Conway, then acting as clerk of the Committee of Investigation, and two of the witnesses. They announced it also as their intention not to let a single Free-soiler escape.

Among all the scenes of violence I witnessed, it is remarkable that the offending parties were invariably on the Pro-slavery side. The Free-state men appeared to me to be intimidated and overawed, in consequence, not merely of the determination and defiant boldness of their opponents, but still more through the sanction given to these acts by the Government.

I often heard the remark, that they would resist, but that they were resolved not to bring themselves into collision with the Federal power. The policy of the Free-state party, prior to the 21st May, was one of determined non-resistance, the people being counselled to give no ground of offence or pretext for violence, and to seek a restoration of justice and order through legal redress alone. That this was the spirit in which they acted, is very evident from the documents and public appeals which issued from them at that period. These documents indicate, indeed, a degree of submission which it is difficult to reconcile with a proper independence, and which gives some colour to the charge often brought against the Free-state men by their opponents, that they were "a set of cowards, who, when it came to fighting, would be certain to give in."

Their later conduct, however, was different. In the hands of their oppressors all justice had been set at defiance. They had been driven out of house and home by an armed mob, acting under territorial authority. The Federal power had been appealed to in vain. The Free-state men were driven to desperation. It was but natural that some revulsion of feeling should be experienced. As it was, guerrilla parties were organized by some of the less passive spirits on the Free-state side, corresponding with those already existing amongst their opponents. These thought themselves justified in recovering stolen horses and other property. Other acts of retaliation occurred. In several instances the opposing parties came into collision, and violence ensued. For some time, therefore, after the attack upon Lawrence, an irregular strife was maintained, and a bitter remembrance filled each man's mind, and impelled to daily acts of hostility and not unfrequent bloodshed.

CHAPTER VI.

Why are such Outrages permitted ?—Total Failure of Justice.
—The Jeffreys of the Territory.—A Test required.—An im-
pious Oath.—Affirmation of the Nebraska-Kansas Act and
the Fugitive Slave Law.—Judge, Jury, and Law.—All one
Way.—Sample of the Kansas Statutes.—Ball and Chain.—
Freedom of Speech forbidden.—Punishment of Death.—
Abuse of the Term "Law."—No Hope of Justice for Free-
state Men.

EACH party in Kansas lays claim to the title
of "law-abiding and order-loving." The Pro-
slavery party, being in power, especially boasts
of its affection for "law and order," and
preaches to its political opponents submission
to the constituted authorities.

Yet the brief history of the territory has
been little else than a succession of unjust oppressions and violent usurpations. It has
been the holiday of crime and wrong, anarchy
and bloodshed. Month after month, English-
men living in their peaceful homes have been
startled by the intelligence of new oppressions

and new outrages committed in Kansas, until they have begun to ask, Are these events occurring in a civilized land? Does the country really possess a government? Is it true that it is under the direct control of the Congress of the United States? Has it really its Governor and Secretary, its Chief Justice and Associate Judges, its Marshals and Sheriffs, its laws and law-officers, of which we read, or are these mere empty titles? In general, how are the extraordinary anomalies, which a condition of affairs like that in Kansas implies, to be accounted for? How comes it that such enormities are permitted? Why is not a remedy applied?

To the solution of such inquiries I propose to devote the present and succeeding chapter.

The first and most natural question is, If such fearful outrages, as every mail brings us intelligence of, are being committed in Kansas, why are not the perpetrators of these enormities brought to justice? Is there no judge, no jury, no law, to which appeal can be made for protection?

The answer is simple. First, the man is

wanting who possesses boldness or rashness enough to bring the offending parties to justice. Murder and cold-blooded assassination were of almost daily occurrence at the time of my visit; but whoever should dare to report such a case would be at once a marked man, and his life, in all probability, before the day had expired, would be the penalty for his imprudence in the cause of right.

But, supposing the offender to be brought to justice, who is the judge, of what character the jury, and what the law by which he has to be tried?

The judge would be such a man as Chief Justice Lecompte—the Jeffreys of the territory. Or, if not the chief of the "bloody assizes" of Kansas, it would be some other minion of the slave power, panting after the extermination of every Free-state advocate, and pledged by his oath of office to sustain the most offensive measures which the slave power has introduced. It cannot be otherwise, for all the public offices are occupied by most resolute adherents of the pro-slavery cause; and, lest any one of a different stamp should creep in, a test is demanded, contrary to the constitution of the United States, of every candidate for office, according to which he is required to subscribe an oath, "solemnly swearing upon the Holy Evangelists of Almighty God," that he will "support and sustain the provisions of the act entitled 'An Act to Organize the Territories of Nebraska and Kansas,' and the provisions of the law of the United States commonly known as the 'Fugitive Slave Law.'" —(*Vide* "Statutes of the Territory of Kansas," page 438.) Thus, by the law of the territory, no man can sit on the bench, or hold any other public office, unless he have first specially indorsed and pledged himself to sustain the two most extreme pro-slavery measures that can possibly be cited.

If such be the judge, the jury would also be of a character no less accurately defined by statute. What is the law of Kansas concerning jurors? "No person who is conscientiously opposed to the holding of slaves, or who does not admit the right to hold slaves in this territory, shall be a juror in any cause in which the right to hold any person in slavery is involved, nor in any cause in which any injury done to, or committed by, any slave is in issue, nor in any criminal proceeding for the violation of any law enacted for the protection of slave property, and for the punishment of crime committed against the right to such property."—(Statutes of Kansas, p. 378.) Again, by the first section of the act, the power is placed in the hands of the "Marshal, Sheriff, or other officer, to summon a sufficient number of jurors."—(p. 377.) And who are Marshal and Sheriff? Donaldson and his deputy Fain are the former; Samuel Jones is the most noted of the latter: together, the destroyers of Lawrence, and the hunters of Free-state men, even to the death. With such a law, and with a discretionary power vested in such hands, it will be seen at once what kind of jury must, of necessity, be procured.

And if such be the character of judge and jury, what are the laws they have to dispense? Take a sample:

"If any person print, write, introduce into, publish, or circulate, or cause to be brought into, printed, written, published, or circulated, or shall knowingly aid or assist in bringing into, printing, publishing, or circulating, within this territory, any book, paper, pamphlet, magazine, hand-bill, or circular, containing any statements, arguments, opinions, sentiment, doctrine, advice, or innuendo, calculated to produce a disorderly, dangerous, or rebellious disaffection among the slaves in this territory, or to induce such slaves to escape from the service of their masters, or to resist their authority, he shall be guilty of felony, and be punished by imprisonment at hard labor for a term of not less than five years."—(Statutes, cap. 151, sec. 11.)

"If any free person, by speaking or writing, assert or maintain that persons have not the right to hold slaves in this territory, or shall introduce into this territory, print, publish, write, circulate, or cause to be introduced into this territory, written, printed, published, or circulated in this territory, any book, paper, magazine, pamphlet, or circular, containing any denial of the right of persons to hold slaves in this territory, such person shall be deemed guilty of felony, and punished by imprisonment at hard labor for a term of not less than two years."—(Statutes, cap. 151, sec. 12.)

And what kind of hard labour is the North-

ern man to undergo who should be lucklessly
brought before a Kansas judge and convict-
ed of denying the right to hold slaves in the
territory? This is defined in the same code,
where, after providing that every person so sentenced shall be deemed a convict, and shall be
put to hard labour on the streets, roads, public
buildings, or other public works of the territory, the act continues :—

" And the keeper shall cause such convict,
while engaged in such labour, to be securely
confined by a chain six feet in length, of not
less than 4-16ths nor more than 3-8ths of an
inch links, with a round ball of iron of not
less than four nor more than six inches in diameter attached, which chain shall be securely
fastened to the ankle of such convict with a
strong lock and key ; and such keeper or other
person having charge of such convict may, if
necessary, confine such convict while so engaged at hard labour, by other chains or other
means, in his discretion, so as to keep such
convict secure and prevent his escape ; and
when there shall be two or more convicts
under the charge of such keeper or other person, such convicts shall be fastened together
by strong chains, with strong locks and keys,

during the time such convicts shall be engaged in hard labour without the walls of any jail or prison".—(Statutes, cap. 22, sec. 2.)

Further, the convict may be "employed upon private hiring at labour" for the benefit of the territorial treasury (cap. 22, sec. 3). The person who gives utterance to a free thought, therefore, may be placed at the will of the Pro-slavery rulers, at the side, if they please, of their negro slaves, to labour in their fields or elsewhere, whilst they drag after them the heavy ball and chain, symbol of their subjection to the slave power.

For greater " offences against slave property" the law provides, of course, a severer penalty. To aid in any rebellion of slaves against their masters, to bring into the territory any book or tract calculated to excite rebellion on the part of slaves, free negroes, or mulattoes, to carry out of the territory a slave belonging to another, or to assist in the same, are all capital offences, to be punished by death.

The man, therefore, who possesses a copy of " Uncle Tom's Cabin" is, in Kansas, on a par with the murderer. His guilt demands the heaviest penalty the law can inflict. But without arguing from cases so extreme, let it be remembered that the utterance of even a syllable against the right of holding slaves is made punishable by two years' imprisonment and hard labour on the public roads, with a chain of six feet and a round ball of iron attached to the ankle, and it will at once be seen whether the law was made for the Pro-slavery or for the Free-state men. Add to this the fact that every act of the Free-state party, if viewed in the light of the laws as interpreted by the Federal government, is an act of treason against the Federal power, and it will be perceived what opportunity is given for the most cruel despotism and the grossest wrong to take refuge in the name and under the sanction of the law. "Law," in fact, was the word constantly in the mouths of the self-styled border ruffians, with whom I myself came daily into contact in Kansas. So far from not appealing to it, everything they did, every enormity they committed, was done in the name of the law of the land. The constant taunt thrown out

against the Free-state party, and the chief difficulty they themselves experienced, was the opposition in which they stood to the recognized
law. "Law and order" became the watch-word
and war-cry of the most lawless in the territory;
and the words "a posse of law-and-order men"
were synonymous with a company of freebooters
and murderers ranging the country in search
of their political opponents. The law, therefore,
was all on one side. And it will be seen that,
with enactments demanding the conviction of
all who spoke or acted against slavery, and a
judge and jury no less desiring their extermination, the wronged Free-state man, though he
should have been struck down in the highway
and robbed of his all, had more to lose than
gain by a recourse to the legal power.

CHAPTER VII.

Southern Law-makers.—Perversion of Authority.—A fraudulent Legislature in Power.—The "Blue Lodge."—The Electors overawed.—General Stringfellow's Speech.—The Physical Force Argument.—How to get a Majority.—Illegal Votes.—Not Four per Cent. Legal.—Terrorism.—Polling.—The Congress Report.—Right of Might.—A forcible Persuader.—Conclusions of the Committee of Investigation.—A Poll-tax.—Pro-Slavery Votes purchasable by Law.—Anti-Slavery Votes pronounced void by Law.—Public Documents cited.—Laws worse than Draconian.

THE reader may be tempted further to ask, how laws so glaringly unreasonable and unjust as those cited in the preceding chapter could have become the laws of the land? By what power or authority were they enacted?

Answer.—They were enacted by a falsely chosen but authoritatively recognized Territorial Legislature. This Legislature, viewed by the general Government as the voice of the people, becomes, of necessity, lawgiver to the people of the territory; and not only gives the laws, but assumes to itself the right to define its own authority. In this way the legal existence of this assembly as a legislative body has been determined by itself, and, being backed by the United States troops, the so-called Kansas Legislature has had almost all power in its own hands. This is the Legislature for which the votes were taken on the 30th of March, 1855, and which, first meeting at Pawnee, was afterwards removed to the Shawnee Mission, to be more conveniently near the Missouri border. It is true, the election was repudiated as fraudulent and unfair by the Free-state population, and that they acted independently of it in causing a fresh election to take place on the 9th of October, 1855. This resulted in the convention for organizing a State Government, which met at Topeka, and the subsequent election of State officers and members of the General Assembly. When this Assembly met the second time at Topeka, on the 4th of July last, it will be remembered that Colonel Sumner forcibly dissolved the Assembly at the head of a considerable body of United States troops, at the same time indicating his own view of the proceeding by stating that it was " the most painful duty of his whole life." Repudiated, however, as the " bogus" Legislature is on the part of the whole Free-state population, it still maintains its power, and gives laws to the territory.

But how, it may next be asked, is this charge established, of the Legislature to which the Federal Government gives the sanction of its approval and the aid of its troops, being thus falsely and fraudulently chosen ?

This fact admits of very easy proof. Long before the first election in Kansas, a secret society had been in existence in Missouri, generally known as the " Blue Lodge," the avowed purpose of which was, by a systematic organization, to control the elections in Kansas. By this agency immense armed bands of men from Missouri were poured into Kansas, and, under the generalship of efficient leaders, so distributed through the electoral districts as to outnumber and overawe the resident voters. The character of these men may be inferred from an address delivered by one of their chief leaders, General Stringfellow, of Weston, in Missouri. General Stringfellow is the brother of the Speaker in

the Legislative Assembly. The style of his
address is very characteristic.

" I tell you to mark every scoundrel among
you that is the least tainted with free-soilism
or abolitionism, and exterminate him. Neither
give nor take quarter from the —— rascals.
I propose to mark them in this house, and on
the present occasion, so you may crush them
out. To those who have qualms of conscience
as to violating laws, state or national, the time
has come when such impositions must be disregarded, as your rights and property are in
danger ; and I advise you, one and all, to enter
every election district in Kansas, in defiance of
Reeder and his vile myrmidons, and vote at
the point of the bowie-knife and the revolver.
Neither give nor take quarter, as our case demands it. It is enough that the slaveholding
interest wills it, from which there is no appeal.
What right has Governor Reeder to rule Missourians in Kansas? His proclamation and
prescribed oath must be repudiated. It is
your interest to do so. Mind that slavery is
established where it is not prohibited."

And as their leader advised them so they
did. They neither gave nor took quarter ; they
allowed no qualms of conscience as to violating

laws ; and they entered every electoral district in Kansas, and, in defiance of the rightful governor, voted at the point of the bowie-knife and the revolver. The result was a majority, almost as ten to one, in favour of the pro-slavery candidate, General Whitfield. Exact returns from each district have since been obtained by the Committee of Investigation, and from their report presented to Congress, I will extract one or two examples of the fraud practised by this invading army.

The seventh district is a remote settlement, as yet very sparsely inhabited, and containing by census not more than 53 voters. In this district alone no less than 597 votes were cast for Whitfield, and seven for another candidate, making in all 604, of which it has been ascertained that not more than 20 were legal, the remaining 584 being consequently illegal votes. In the eleventh district, Marysville, " the total number of white inhabitants, including men, women, and children, was 36, of whom 24 were voters. Yet the poll-lists in this district show that 245 votes were cast at this election ! * * * By a comparison of the census-roll with the poll-books it appears that but seven resident settlers voted; and 238 votes were illegally and fraudulently given!"

And what was done at the election of a delegate to Congress was repeated at the election of the members of the Legislative Assembly. By the report of the Committee of Investigation it appears that the proportion of illegal to legal votes was as 4,908 to 1,410! From the census it appears there were but 2,905 voters in the whole Territory, yet 5,427 votes were recorded on the Pro-slavery side alone! Many of the Missourians returned the same night, after giving their vote, to their own State. At Leavenworth, a great number came down by steamboat from Weston, and having effected their object, returned by the same boat. Many affirmed their right to vote as residents, although they might have been only an hour in the territory, and had their home in Missouri. The enormities committed by these armed bands were fearful. Some we read of standing around the polling-place and saying that "no difficulty would be made if they were allowed to vote in peace, but that they were determined to vote anyhow, and that each one of them was prepared for eight rounds without loading, and would go to the ninth round with the butcher-knife." If the judges who presided over the elections refused to receive their votes without administering the oath of residence, the Missourian invaders held their pistols at their heads, while they appointed fresh judges from their own number, and proceeded with the election, "masters of the position." So violent was their hatred to the oath, that any voter who professed himself ready to take it was threatened with instant death, amid cries of " Shoot him !" " Cut his guts out !" &c. " One of them," we read in the report of the commissioners,

" Mr. J. N. Mace, was asked if he would take the oath ; and, upon his replying that he would if the judges required it, he was dragged through the crowd away from the polls amidst cries of ' Kill the —— nigger thief,' ' Cut his throat,' ' Tear his heart out,' &c. After they got him to the outside of the crowd, they stood around him with cocked revolvers and drawn bowie-knives ; one man putting a knife to his breast so that it touched him ; another holding a cocked pistol to his ear, while another struck at him with a club."

The whole of the voluminous evidence accompanying the report submitted to Congress goes to establish a succession of similar enormities in each of the polling districts. These investigations were being carried on within two doors of the place where I was myself staying when in Leavenworth; and it was sufficient to hear the manner in which the Missourians affirmed their right to come over from their own State and vote in the Territory of Kansas, and their determination to do so on every occasion and at all hazards, to understand the violence with which they would assert that right when confronted with their political opponents at the polling-places.

Another question may be suggested on this topic. By what right do these Missourians or others from the neighbouring States vote in the Kansas elections?

By no right whatever except that of might. The Missourians have no more right to vote in Kansas than the voters in Middlesex have, after using their rightful suffrage in their own county, to go with their knives into Surrey and record their votes a second time, with a pistol at the head of the election officer, in order to control the Surrey elections. Indeed, as the States of the Union are by their constitution perfectly independent of one another and self-governed, the parallel would be truer if we were to picture an army of Frenchmen, larger in number than the aggregate of all our voters, who should, at the point of the sword, choose for us our representatives, and return without exception as our rulers men from among themselves or pledged to their own political sentiments.

So much was it an act of main force and illegal oppression, that among the conclusions which the Commissioners of Investigation report as established by the testimony adduced, they give the first place to the following :—

"That each election in the Territory, held under the organic or alleged Territorial law, has been carried by organized invasion from the State of Missouri, by which the people of the Territory have been prevented from exercising the rights secured to them by the organic law."

And as being the fruit of an organized invasion they conclude,—

" Secondly, that the alleged Territorial Legislature was an illegally constituted body, and had no power to pass valid laws, and their enactments are therefore null and void."

While, however, in the first instances, the interference of the Missourians was wholly illegal, the Legislature thus illegally constituted took care to legalize the act for the future. Hence we find them enacting in the " Act instituting a poll-tax :"—

" Sect. 1. That every free white male above the age of twenty-one years who shall pay to the proper officer in Kansas Territory the sum of one dollar as a poll-tax, and shall produce to the judges of any election within and for the Territory of Kansas a receipt showing the payment of said poll-tax, shall be deemed a legal voter, and shall be entitled to vote at any election in said Territory during the year for which the same shall have been paid, provided that the right of suffrage shall be exercised only by citizens of the United States and those who have declared on oath their intention to become such, and shall have taken an oath to support the constitution of the United States and the provisions of the act organizing the Territory of Kansas."

In other words, by the payment of a single dollar any citizen of any one of the United States can purchase a voting power in Kansas for a twelvemonth, provided he pledges himself to the support of the Organic Act. In contrast to this, in the 11th section (Statutes, p. 282) it is expressly enacted that while every inhabitant of Kansas paying a territorial tax is a qualified elector, yet should he, on being challenged to take an oath to sustain the provisions of the Nebraska-Kansas Bill and the Fugitive Slave Law, "refuse to take such oath or affirmation, the vote of such person shall be rejected."

Hence, in the election of members for the new Legislature, the results of which we recently received, the pro-slavery Missourian who paid a dollar was entitled to a vote, while the Free-state settler in Kansas, though an owner of land in the Territory, was denied his right of suffrage by the Territorial law. The same law required the candidates also, in order to be eligible at that election, to take oath in support of the Fugitive Slave Law (Statutes, p. 332). The prediction, therefore, as to the results of the election, which was ventured when these facts were first laid before the English public, was one in relation to which no room for speculation could be said to exist. The complete verification of it in the return of a wholly pro-slavery Legislature, of which we have recently received the intelligence, was the only result which could reasonably be anticipated.

At the risk of writing that which is less generally interesting, I have presented in this and the preceding chapter numerous extracts from public documents. I have deemed it right to do this, because the whole value of the present statements rests on the authority whence they are derived. The references I have made are, firstly, to the " Statutes of the Territory of Kansas," issued by the legislative body, to which, though chosen by the inhabitants of another State, the Government at Washington gives the sanction of its approval and its military aid; and, secondly, to the report and evidence of " the Special Committee appointed to investigate the troubles in the Territory of

Kansas"—a report which, though dissented from by one member of the committee, contains testimony which can never be overthrown or gainsaid.

My simple object has been to show that the dark deeds of which I was an eye-witness in Kansas, some of which I have detailed in former chapters, are no darker than the public acts of the slave-power in that territory, as exhibited in the archives of its House of Assembly ; and that the fearful anarchy and unrestrained lawlessness which reign throughout the territory find both their parallel and their key in the flagrant unrighteousness of their legal enactments.

CHAPTER VIII.

Recapitulation.—The " bogus" Legislature.—Men and Things
in Kansas.—Different Classes of Settlers.—Immense Extent
of Country.—Physical Aspect.—Rivers.—The Kansas and
Missouri.—Undulating Prairie.— Caravans.—Indian Tribes.
—Fertility of the Soil.—Salubrity of the Climate.—Commercial Advantages.—The " mad Missouri." —Excellent
Market.—" Nebraska-Kansas Act."—A Race between North
and South.—Pro-slavery Party in the Ascendant.—Struggle
between the two Parties.—Tarring and Feathering.—Sale
of a Free Man.—Model Legislators.—Discordant Elements.
—Development.

IN my earlier chapters on the subject of Kansas, I attempted to depict some of the scenes
of riot and exhibitions of maddened hostility
which fell within my own experience as a
traveller in that territory immediately after
the burning and sack of the town of Lawrence.
In others I have endeavoured to explain the
extraordinary fact of such lawlessness being permitted, by showing from the statute-books of
the territory that such acts were not the fruit
of a sudden and exceptional outbreak of pas-

sion, but were the reflection of the deliberate injustice of their legislative enactments. I have also indicated the fact that the Legislature, which has thus shamefully abused its power, is not the choice of the people of Kansas, but mainly of the inhabitants of an adjoining State, who controlled the elections by entering and voting in the territory in far larger number than the total of its own voting population. Further, that this Legislature—commonly called a "bogus," that is, a spurious Legislature—possesses the sanction of the general Government, and the aid, consequently, of the United States' troops. On the same ground, every act of the people of Kansas to gain for themselves a true representation and a better government is regarded as "treason" or "rebellion;" and the leaders of such "rebellion" have, as in the instance of General Robinson and others, suffered, although untried, a long and painful imprisonment.

This fact of an unrepresented minority, or, with more truth, an unrepresented majority of the people of Kansas, is alone sufficient to shield the settlers in that territory from the charge of universally participating in this system of legalized ruffianism. There are, in truth, large numbers of people occupying claims in the territory, whose sole purpose evidently is to act as peaceful pioneers of civilization by transforming the rich prairie lands of Kansas into a home for themselves and their children. In justice to these and all others concerned, I purpose devoting one or two chapters to a description of men and things generally in Kansas; comprehending, if possible, some description of the external aspect of the country, its towns and cultivation, with a more special portraiture of the classes of men there to be met—the Western settler, the Free-state advocate, the Southern planter, the border-man, and all other varieties of inhabitant that constitute the existing elements of Kansas society. This may meet the wants of those whose interest in the political struggle, of which Kansas is the theatre, may lead them to inquire what kind of appearance the place presents, and what objects meet the eye of one travelling in that distant territory.

And first, in addition to that which Kansas

has of its own, those characteristics must be presupposed which it possesses in common with all the other vast territories of the American " far West." There is immense extent of country. Add together England, Wales, Scotland, and Ireland, and the aggregate superficies will yield almost precisely the area of Kansas; which, nevertheless, is small compared with its sister territory, Nebraska. There is interest attached to its physical aspect. Rivers of immense proportions roll their vast and muddy volume along, ordinarily at a great depth beneath the elevation of the general surface, through which they have cut their deep broad channel, leaving a margin of high bluffs, sometimes covered with a thick growth of cottonwood and elm,—at others too steep to admit of more than the scantiest vegetation. Near these rivers, and especially on the borders of the Kansas and Missouri, are fine bottom-lands covered with a rich and most fertile soil, needing nothing but the plough to convert them into fruitful fields. Then follows prairie—beautiful, undulating prairie—here and there a grove of walnut, hickory, oak, or sugar-maple, but for

the most part a broad treeless and shrubless
pasturage, stretching its velvety surface of grass
as far as the horizon, decked, too, at the spring
season—when I saw it—with prairie flowers of
every hue, and alive with the hum of insects
no less variegated in colour and delicate in form.
Let the traveller put himself upon one of the
trails joining the caravan for Santa Fé, or
Oregon, or Utah, and he may spend his month
or six weeks amid the monotony of this sea of
grass as on an ocean voyage, traversing the
green waves of its rolling surface, with a circular
horizon always around him, till, having crossed
twelve and a half degrees of longitude, he finds
himself at the foot of the Rocky Mountains, and
at length at the western boundary of Kansas.
With the exception, however, of these trains,
which pass and repass with their long waggons
and innumerable oxen during the summer
months, the broad prairie-lands of Central and
Western Kansas are left to the occupancy of
the wandering tribes of Indians, of whom it has
been estimated that there are yet 25,000 in the
territory; while the better-watered, better-
wooded, and more fertile lands in the East are

occupied by the 10,000, or more, belligerent settlers of our own blood, of whom we have heard so much.

Were there nothing else to attract settlers but the fertility of the land, the salubrity of the climate, and the commercial advantages it possesses, Kansas would still have been sought out as a favourable spot for Western emigrants. Its soil, so far as I had opportunity to observe it, in the lands watered by the Kansas and Missouri rivers, is as rich as in any part of the whole West of the United States, admirably adapted for pasturage, suitable for Indian corn and other crops, and, in some parts, for the cultivation of hemp or tobacco. Its climate, hot in summer, is nevertheless healthy, and free, according to all accounts, from the fever and ague so prevalent in many parts of Missouri. Its economical advantages are quite peculiar. It is, by virtue of its situation, the key to all the vast territory which, westward and northward, opens out from the junction of the Kansas and Missouri rivers. The Kansas itself is no inconsiderable stream. It receives into it the Smoky-hill, the Grand Saline, Solomon's, and

the Republican Forks, besides smaller tributaries, each of these greater in length, and in
the spring very much larger in volume, than
our own Thames. The "mad" Missouri, although having more than 1,600 miles to run
when it passes Leavenworth before it reaches
the sea, and having already traversed 2,600
miles since it left the Great Falls, is, for the
whole distance, open to steam navigation;
while above the Falls the stream may still be
navigated by smaller craft for hundreds of
miles towards its source in the Rocky Mountains. But, independently of this prospective
commerce, the settler in Eastern Kansas already
possesses the advantage of water communication
by which at once to forward his produce to the
southern market, and, above all, an excellent
market at his own door in the necessities of
produce and of stock arising from the constant
fitting out of the trains for New Mexico, which
make the cities on the Kansas border their
starting-place and entrepôt.

But with much in these respects to attract
the settler, Kansas owes, doubtless, the rapidity
of its settlement principally to the political

interests which have gathered around it. From the first moment when the Nebraska-Kansas Act was passed, which, whilst it organized Kansas into a Territory, swept away all former stipulations as to the exclusion of slavery, it was perceived alike by North and South that the future of Kansas in relation to slavery, and with it, probably, of all territories that might afterwards be admitted, must be determined by the numerical proportions of its population. A race was commenced between North and South, and that party was to be the winner who should send in the largest number of its own adherents, whether Free-state men or pro-slavery men, to determine the law for the new Territory. Measures were taken by the pro-slavery party to prevent the allotment of lands to any but their own partisans; and when Free-state men still came in, squatter meetings were held in Kansas by inhabitants of Missouri, who passed resolutions to the following effect:

" That we will afford protection to no abolitionist as a settler on this Territory.

" That we recognize the institution of slavery

as already existing in this Territory, and advise slaveholders to introduce their property as early as possible."

To meet these efforts on the part of organizations in Missouri, Emigrant Aid societies were formed in Boston and elsewhere in the Eastern States to promote the movement on the side of the North, and to give facilities to settlers intending to make Kansas their home. That these were *bonâ fide* settlers, and not an invading army of illegal voters like the Missourians, we have abundant proof. Indeed, it is idle to suppose that men went from Boston to Kansas, an overland journey equalling in distance that from London to Odessa, their expenses not being paid by the society, merely with a view to record their votes, and then return.

The two parties, as might be anticipated, soon came to blows. Public meetings were perpetually being held, secret committees formed, political clubs organized. A single instance selected out of many will illustrate the operation of these hostile measures.

A Vigilance Committee was appointed in the spring of 1855, having for its object " to observe and report all such persons as shall, * * * by the expression of abolition sentiments, produce disturbance to the quiet of the citizens or danger to their domestic relations; and all such persons so offending shall be notified and made to leave the territory." On this committee were several members of the Legislature. The first person "observed and reported" by the committee as acting so as to endanger " their domestic relations" (by which delicate expression is meant the institution of slavery) was Mr. William Phillips, a lawyer residing in Leavenworth, whose offence was that he had sworn to a protest against the validity of the election in his district, in consequence of which protest Governor Reeder had ordered a new election. Mr. Phillips was "notified" to leave the territory. He refused to do so, whereupon he was seized by a party of Missouri men to the number of fourteen, taken across the river, and carried several miles into Missouri. They then proceeded to shave one side of his head, next stripped off his clothes, and put him through the horrible ordeal of tarring and feathering. This being completed, they rode him on a rail for a mile and a-half, and finally put him up at auction, a negro acting as auctioneer, and went through the mockery of selling him, not at the price of a slave, but for the sum of one dollar. Eight days after this outrage a public meeting was held, at which the following resolution was unanimously adopted: " That we heartily endorse the action of the committee of citizens that shaved, tarred and feathered, rode on a rail, and had sold by a negro, William Phillips, the moral perjurer." The meeting was presided over by Mr. Rees, a member of Council in the Kansas Legislature, and the resolution was offered by Mr. Payne, a Judge and also member of the House of Representatives! The outrage committed against Mr. Phillips was not, therefore, the hasty act of a few murderous ruffians, but one advisedly carried out and afterwards deliberately endorsed by a number of citizens and by members of both Houses of Legislature. Mr. Phillips returned to Leavenworth, but has since, according to accounts received in the autumn of 1856, been shot.

To return, however, from this digression. It was out of elements thus discordant that the social life of Kansas had to develope itself. The settler from the North brought his shrewd intelligence and hard-working industry; the man of the South his fearless spirit and cavalier independence. Both were animated by a determination to conquer. United they might have made of Kansas a garden of plenty and an advance-post of civilization. But their work in the territory was to oppose one another. And, although this might have been done by pacific means, yet, differing widely as they did in natural characteristics, in their sympathies and their political aims, they soon yielded to the influence of party bitterness, so that the Northern man's persevering energy and the Southerner's high-spirited daring found exercise, not in furthering a common cause, but in acts of mutual hostility.

CHAPTER IX.

Striking Contrast.—Freedom and Slavery.—Rapid Progress of Kansas.—Northern Emigrant Aid Societies.—Spirit of Enterprise.—The "Regulators."—"Law and Order" Men.—The Widow's Son.—Barbarous Outrage.—The Western Frontiersman.—His character.—Generous Reciprocity.—Mode of Intercourse.—The Pioneer of the New World.—His Appointments.—The Romance of Peril.—Achievements of the Western Pathfinder.—Contempt of the Yankees.—The Source of Life and Vigour.—Effect of Politics on the Western Character.

NOWHERE in America, probably, is the contrast between the Northern and the Southern man exhibited in so marked a manner as in Kansas. He who would see the difference between comfort and discomfort, between neatness and disorder, cleanliness and filth, between farming the land and letting the land farm itself, between trade and stagnation, stirring activity and reigning sloth, between a wide-spread intelligence and an almost universal ignorance, between general progress and an incapacity for all improvement or advancement, has commonly only to cross the border-line which separates a free from a slave State. But he who would see these broad contrasts in a single view, the evidences of well-directed enterprise and intelligent energy mixed up with the ugly features of backgoing and barbarity, should seek out Kansas and make its strange varieties of inhabitants his study.

Kansas is not altogether bad. It has its redeeming features, its fairer as well as its darker aspects, as if to justify Byron's line,—"None are all evil." An impulse more than ordinary has been given on the part of the North, and the necessities of the settler have been more than ordinarily anticipated. Usually life in the bush or life on the prairie implies a long apprenticeship of toil before the reward of industry is reached. The Western settler must in most instances make up his mind to years of lonely struggle, hard battling with the earth and elements, before he finds himself surrounded by the life of civilization even in its most rudimentary forms. But it has not been wholly so in

Kansas. The want of capital, which is a principal source of the difficulties and embarrassments that so long retard the progress of settler in a new country, has been in a great degree met by the active exertions of the Northern emigrant-aid societies. The appliances of civilized life are, as a consequence, by no means wanting. The church, the school-house, the public hall, the necessities of commerce, sawmills, and other erections of industry, are all in a certain degree provided; and large public works and costly undertakings are promised, and already have an existence on paper, which are in advance of the wants of the place for many years to come. Hence, trade has been greatly stimulated and a degree of enterprise developed which, had not the pursuits of industry been diverted by the rude checks of war, would have made this new territory remarkable in the annals of successful progress and rapid increase.

Unfortunately, as I had too many proofs at the time of my visit, the labours of the honest and well-disposed among the settlers were most grievously interfered with by the necessity of bearing arms and shielding themselves from political oppression. The farmers were neglecting their corn fields to form committees of defence. Others found themselves mercilessly robbed of their produce and of their horses and other stock, to supply the wants of the " Regulators," who, in the name of " law and order," scoured the country in search of political victims. A young man, when I was there, was attacked by a band of men, who demanded his horse. He refused. They held their pistols before him, and renewed the demand: "He must give his horse, or drop." He again asserted his right to his own. The "Regulators" were firm. He pleaded, if not justice, mercy— telling them that he was the only son of a widowed mother, and that to take his horse would be to rob him of his chief means of supporting, not himself alone, but her. The "Law-and-Order" men were weary of the discussion. A single shot terminated both it and the young man's life.

But where these acts of violence were not committed, the diversion of the settlers' labour from the cultivation of their farms, to the organ-

izing of means of defence, was sufficient to lead
to serious apprehension as to the consequences.
It was my intention to have referred to this before the sad intelligence arrived that the Free-
state inhabitants of Lawrence were suffering
from scarcity, and that the merchant in Weston
who sold them a quantity of flour had been arrested by a band of men from Platte City, with
the renowned Stringfellow at their head, who
denounced the flour-dealer as an Abolitionist,
and threatened to hang him.   Fortunately, the
people of Weston, who love free-trade, it appears, if they love nothing else that is free, came
to the rescue of their fellow-citizen, and compelled the Platte party to take their departure.

To draw a true picture of Kansas life it is
necessary, of course, to place in the foreground
the true typical Western frontiersman.   Coming
originally, whether from the cultivated farms of
New England or from the broad plantations of
the South, the settler in the West speedily
acquires those general characteristics which
belong to the border, and which mark out the
Western man as of a species distinct from either
Northerner or Southerner.   It would be diffi-

cult, perhaps, to define it precisely, but there is an element in the Western character which, in the case of the majority I believe of our own countrymen, would gain for it their natural sympathies more readily than they are yielded to the Eastern inhabitants of the States, either North or South.   This is the secret, probably, of that strange attraction which belongs, notwithstanding all its discomforts and all its perils, to the border life of the furthest West. Placed in circumstances where they have to endure frequent hardship and privation, called oftentimes to encounter great danger, and to expose their lives to the most imminent perils, these hardy men become in a short time wholly indifferent to all considerations of personal comfort or safety.   By a natural transition they are next found deriving pride and pleasure from the life of hardship to which they have become inured, despising the softness of civilization and conventional society, and loving only the proud independence and excitement of a life, in which the surmounting of obstacles, the subduing of nature and perpetual hair-breadth escapes, form the chief staple of each day's experience.

Further, the border-man is so situated with
regard to his fellow settler that he is most
naturally led to share all he has with his neighbour, and to make common stock of whatever
little conveniences each can afford.   If A is
felling timber, he will cut for B too, who lives
in the log-house four miles off, and who perhaps has unfortunately lost or broken his axe;
and if B's wife has got a saucepan, A's better-
half shall not want the means wherewithal to
prepare the " hog and hominy" for the family's
wants.   And why not ?   If there were no
such generous interchange, a weary week's
journey might need to be undertaken before
Mr. B could replace his axe or Mrs. A her
saucepan.   A Western man will take no re-
compense for services rendered, however kind
or valuable ; he dislikes to be offered thanks.
In my own experience, the most simple ac-
knowledgment of favour by a plain " if you
please," or " I thank you," has been received
with very evident displeasure that I should
introduce the coldness of Eastern conventional-
ism to mar the freedom of friendly intercourse.
The most unbounded hospitality reigns, the

talk of the stranger and the news he may
bring being the set-off against all he may receive. This set-off, however, he must give;
for the Western man, while he holds that you
have a free right to everything in his cabin
without asking so much as his permission, considers that you and yours are equally at his
disposal, and that, should he detain you for a
night beneath his roof, you are bound to answer every one of the endless questions he has
to present for your solution. Whatever is not
generous and free, the true border-man with
difficulty comprehends and most heartily hates.
Let the stranger leave behind him all home
prejudices, all the chill formalities of conventional society—be ready to accept the rough
fare set before him, which, if not good, is yet
the best the country will afford—show no fear,
no suspicion, no restraint—handle his rifle as if
it were his cherished companion—be hearty
and cheerful and ready to communicate, not in
word only, but by handing out his brandy-flask,
or participating anything else he may have
with his entertainers, without allowing it to
appear in the smallest degree an act of favour,

and tell the rough settler that, though " of Eastern raising," his heart is with the West, and there is not a log-cabin in the whole border-]and from north to south which is not open for his reception. Except in Kansas, one is compelled to add; for there, although the Western nature is still the same—and rightly managed, there is little to fear even from the man who glories in the name of border-ruffian —yet, through this detestable war, the generosity of the Western character is marred, and each man looks with suspicion upon either stranger or neighbour.

It is impossible, however, rightly to comprehend life in Kansas without taking into consideration the natural characteristics of the Western borderer. Take him at his best, and the pioneer of the New World possesses a noble character. There he stands, in his rough woollen shirt of yellow or red, his big boots forming a large circumference around his leath ern hose, a buffalo-skin upon his back—at once his covering by day and his bed, sheet, and blanket all combined by night—his coonskin cap, or slouched felt hat, covering a face which hot suns and keen frosts have made brown as an Indian's, his rifle across his shoulder, powder-horn and shot-pouch hanging from his neck, his belt stuck full of twine and knives, and hatchets and ammunition, and all the minor necessaries of his life—the produce of his last shot perhaps upon his shoulder, his visage the fiercer for uncombed hair and thick bristly beard; there he stands, ready for the widest river, or the thickest forest, or the broadest prairie, or the wildest Indian, or the most savage beast that it may be his lot to light on, ready to do or die.

That there is a charm in all this, at least to "those whose hearts are fresh and simple," and who are sick of the luxury and display, the hollow pretence and unmanly refinements of the Eastern cities, will be understood by every one. There is romance about the unheeded perils and unthought-of hardships, there is attraction in the manly generosity of these brave pioneers of civilization. They are the men to conquer the wild woods and stern nature that is before them; and they do it. Step by step, not gradually, but rapidly, they have carried

forward the outposts of civilized life; the red
man has receded before them; the waste wilderness has been transformed into a fruitful
field; hundreds, thousands of miles have submitted to the steady march of their conquest;
population has followed to fill up from behind
the lands they have cleared; and hating, as
" crowded up like a city," the place where
they can see in the distance the smoke of another man's log-hut, or cross another man's
claim, they ever move on, loving only the act
of conquest, and the pride of giving to the
world new lands for its enjoyment.

Open-hearted, hospitable, manly, enterprising, reckless of danger, careless of comfort, full
of cool courage and determination as the Western pathfinder is, it may readily be supposed he
holds in most hearty contempt the delicately
raised Yankee, that is, inhabitant of the North-
eastern States. To him the Yankee appears
the embodiment of all that is stiff and cold,
calculating and selfish. He would not exchange
the " rough and ready" welcome to one of his
own Western log-huts, for all the gorgeous
saloons and costly display of the most brilliant

receptions in the Eastern cities.   And well it
is that, in some part of the Union, the manly
strength of its first founders is thus perpetua-
ted.   With all his faults, there is life and vigour
in the Western borderer, and although capable
of being transformed into the worst of ruffians,
because the most reckless and determined, yet
there are elements of character, as it has been
my object to show, in this rough population of
Missouri and other border lands, which are
noble in themselves, and of the highest value
to the interests of the States.

How this Western character has been affected by the strife of politics, how it has been
engrafted upon other stocks and transmuted
into new forms, I shall next describe.   But
this subject must be reserved for another chapter, in which I hope to pourtray more particularly the varieties of inhabitants to be met with
in the seat of Western war and thus to place
before English eyes a picture of log-hut life in
Kansas.

CHAPTER X.

THE population of Kansas comprehends various classes of inhabitants, each distinguished from the others by very marked characteristics. Leaving out of view its native Indians, the country cannot be rightly understood, without some apprehension of the varieties of humankind existing among its white settlers.

The company I had on board the steamboat in the ascent of the Missouri, described in an earlier chapter of this book, might be taken as representing not inadequately the various classes of population in Kansas. The loudest men on board—the rulers and men of authority by virtue of noise—were the Missourians and border-ruffians generally. Early or late, in the saloon or on deck, at the bar or in the berths, there was no release from their ceaseless clamour. The rifles on the table or in the corners, and the pistols in their pockets, were so many fresh arguments to strengthen the bravado of their words. No contrary opinion need attempt to stem the torrent of their turbulent bluster. Even so is it in Kansas. The loudest men whose authority is gained by the defiance they bid, revolver in hand, to all opposition, are the supporters of the political views of the South. The majority of these are natives of Missouri, but many whom I met had come from States as distant as Georgia and South Carolina,—to appearance the off-scourings of the population; young men of spirit and fire, whose love of a fight had tempted them to engage in the strife.

Next, there were doubtless among my fellow-passengers silent Free-soilers—so silent as to their views that it would be impossible to identify them, were it not that a Northern man can scarcely conceal his·more unimpassioned manners, his more careful attention to his dress, and his colder and more formal demeanour in general. So, also, is it in Kansas. There are abundant proofs of the existence of quiet and industrious settlers from the North, silently trying to live out the storm, and thus prevent the triumph of a mighty wrong. A considerable portion of these reach Kansas, by a somewhat tedious overland route, through the Northern State of Iowa, to avoid the risk of travelling through a Slave State. This accounts for the fact that, were I to set all cool temperaments and men silent on slavery to the credit of the Free-soilers, that party would still have been very poorly represented among my fellow passengers.

Further, there were on board Spaniards belonging to New Mexico, filthy as to their persons, disgusting in their manners. These, also, form a part of the transient population of Kansas. Moreover, there were several nuns going up to one of the Roman Catholic missions, and some adherents of the Mormon faith, making their way, probably, across the plains to Utah. Besides these were Jews, for the most part of German origin, of whom a large class carry on the trading and storekeeping in the towns of Kansas. There were Germans also—called by the Americans " Dutchmen"—who, intent on making a livelihood, have settled so thickly in Kansas, as they have done in all the Western lands, that there are more German than English names upon the shops and warehouses, and they almost bid fair to monopolize the commerce of the country. Then there were others intent on making gain, but not the honest gain of the German—namely, the professed gamblers. These were men who played a trick with cards, well known on the Western waters, which occupies but a single minute. They never accepted a stake of less than $100. They began their work late at night, and left the boat about daylight, carrying with them many hundreds of dollars which they had got from the drinking, maddened ruffians, fresh from the spoil of Lawrence. These, unfortunately, are too numerously represented also in the Territory. Again, there were of our number agents of the Federal as well as the Territorial Govern-

ment, and officers in the United States' army;
and, lastly, the African race was represented,
not only by the waiters and others employed
on the boat, but also by a poor slave, who, for
safety's sake, was handcuffed, and sat ordinarily
in a corner, where the black barber found for
him a seat, dropping only his wrists between
his knees when a stranger approached, to
hide, apparently, the shameful shackle from his
gaze.

But amid all these—Pro-slavery men, Free-
soilers, New Mexicans, Mormons, Nuns, Jews,
Germans, professional gamblers, Federal officers,
and slaves—there was no liberty of speech, unless the license claimed by the Southern braves
be deemed a species of liberty. In an under-
tone, and keeping to the German language, I
ventured to condemn the existing outrages,
while conversing with two Germans. I found
them of my own mind, but, they added, no one
durst open his mouth. Of the denial of freedom of speech a curious illustration occurred
as our steamer was approaching the border-line
of Kansas. The word "abolition" had unguardedly dropped from the lips of the clerk of the

boat, not with the customary oath, but with a laugh. "Shut up," was the instant rejoinder, proceeding from a gruff, hoarse voice, "reck'n we're in a section now, where you can't say that there word, not even in jest, so don't crowd on so mighty powerful. You'll have to allow to respect the wishes of the sovereign people; it's them that's to rule;—d'ye hear, Mister?"

Another fellow-passenger held the same views. He was a Judge, and resident in Missouri. I forget his name, but it might have been O'Trigger. Judge O'Trigger was one of the best-looking of the Missouri men. He was evidently well to do, and had the respect of the others, forming often the centre of a circle before whom he would deliver his opinions. He was a man of fine frame and handsome appearance —tall, but also stout; his eye betokened determination, and his countenance was not unattractive, albeit his cheek was unceasingly, except at mealtime, distended with the tobacco quid. He was well dressed, wore a "Know-Nothing" hat, and had a black coat on his back, which, however, he removed when he sat down to meals, thus making more conspicuous his tobacco-stained shirt-front.   This worthy judge was a leader of the talk on board, and I believe I owe much of my personal safety to the fact of my not refusing to form one of his circle of auditors.   But let Sir Oracle speak for himself.

"I've got some boys* up hyar, and I expect I'll bring them down.   Reckon property's a 'nation sight safer at home than among those mean, cantankerous Abolition cusses.   That's what I'm goin' up for, gentlemen.   Got a steep lot, I reckon, altogether; but they're no account in these hyar diggins now, with them Abolition rascals; that's a fact."   Next, discoursing on the agitating politics of the day, the subject to which he always reverted, " Tall times these, gentlemen.   Those Massachusetts men calculated they'd have it all their own way, I reckon.   Get us only on their —— tracks.   We'll soon knock the wind out of

---

* By "boys" in the Southern States are meant negroes. The appellation, however, has no reference to age. "Old man" is another frequent form of address, in speaking to negro slaves.

them, that's sartin. What on airth have they to do hyar, I should like to know? Let Massachusetts govern itself, I say; and *we*'ll govern *our*selves. That's so. Let Massachusetts govern itself, and *we*'ll govern *our*selves, I say. That's right and fair; and they've no right to interfere." All joined heartily in admiring the legal wisdom of Judge O'Trigger, interpreting his conclusion as it was meant,—namely, that Missouri should govern Kansas. Then, in order to prevent the intrusion of Massachusetts men, he had his remedy at hand. "We're not agoin' to let them pass in, no how. There's too many in it, by a long sight, a'ready. We're most agen the border now, I reckon. Catch e'er a one of them passing; by ——, if I won't scalp him. There's one thing we'll do. We'll pass the word round the boat at the last landing, so as they can jest kinder have their choice which way they like. They must just be good on the hemp or land. That's how we'll crowd it on 'em, or they'll have to allow to take the change out of this hyar revolver of mine. That's so; they must just be right on the hemp or put ashore. We've stood them a mighty steep time, but they ain't agoin' to carry on that powerful any longer. That's a fact." The judicial functionary repeated many times his plan, whereby to separate the wheat from the chaff among the passengers; but, fortunately, when we reached the boundary line the excitement was too great to admit of its execution. Most probably the whole of it was mere bravado.

CHAPTER XI.

Two great Divisions.—Pro-slavery Men and Free-soilers.—
Subdivisions.—Slaves.—Small Number of Slave-owners in
Kansas.—Their Works.—" Border-ruffians."—King of the
Fire-eaters.—Their Numbers.—Volunteer Companies.—An
American " Groggery."—A Border-ruffian's Boast.—A fair
" Border-ruffian."—The Free-state Party.—General Lane.—
Governor Robinson.—His Services.—Enormities of Naples
and Austria reproduced in America.—Relative Numbers in
Kansas of Southerns and Northerns.—Migration.—Per-
manent Settlers.—Floating Population.—Western Cities.—
Contrast between Free and Slave Towns.

THE two great divisions in the population of
Kansas are, of course, the pro-slavery men and
the free-soilers. These are the two rival armies
which, having poured during the past two years
into the territory, form the bulk of its inhabitants, and now stand side by side contending
for the mastery of power in the future State.
These parties are susceptible also of a sub-divis-
ion, according as their purposes in entering the
territory are peaceable or warlike. A most notable distinction is that which separates the man

who, whatever be the policy he has espoused, seeks to carry the day by his right of suffrage as a permanent honest settler, and the lover of disturbance who comes to assert victory at the expense of falsehood, treachery, robbery, and bloodshed. Judge O'Trigger, who had "got some boys up to Kansas," and who spared executing his threat against those who would not wear the pro-slavery badge, — namely, a bunch of hemp, symbolic of a rope, stuck into the buttonhole — is, thus far, greatly more to be respected than the Northern man who, in the pursuit of his cause, should turn his Yankee acuteness to dishonest account.

There are, therefore, *bona fide* settlers among the pro-slavery men. Judging by the number of slaves, which, according to the census of 1855, was 192, and has not, probably, increased since that time, those who have brought their "live stock" with them, in order to cultivate the soil, are not many. A single Southern planter will often own four or five times the whole number of slaves existing in Kansas. But in the Western States the ownership is generally limited. Supposing, therefore, the average of "hands" owned by one master in Kansas to be as small as four, which my own observation would lead me to think a sufficiently low estimate, we still have fewer than fifty as the total number of slave-owning settlers in Kansas. It is singular that for the sake of fifty men, to protect them in their "right" to hold property in slaves, so many other rights have been trampled under foot, and thousands of honest men interdicted in the peaceful possession of their lands and the legal exercise of their political suffrages. There are, as may be supposed, many besides, who, although not owning slaves, are yet rightful pro-slavery settlers. Still, if we are to estimate their number by the evidences of their industry, and ask what cities have they built, what buildings have they erected, what lands have they brought under culture, what commerce have they introduced, where are their farm-houses in the country, and their stores, and warehouses, and schools, and churches in the towns, we should come to the conclusion that if they are as numerous as they profess to be, their powers are so absorbed by their much talking that they are unable to exhibit any proportionate fruit of the labour of their hands.

Of the pro-slavery men who are not permanent settlers, little need be said.   These are the " border-ruffians," who have figured so much and so ill in the short history of Kansas.   Their acts sufficiently indicate their character.   Bold, reckless men, intent upon one object, and that the extermination of every Free-soiler from the territory, utterly unscrupulous as to the means by which their object shall be attained, they are to be seen and heard on every side — now standing in knots at the street corners, or in the bar-rooms, concocting their schemes of strife ; now as marauding "posses," armed to the teeth, galloping across the country, ready to waylay and hang on the nearest tree any one they may meet who will not join their faction ; again, in large numbers assembling in some "grocery," surrounded by whisky and rum barrels, or in the open air, addressed by some one of their leading men, some king of the " Fire-eaters," who makes them swear to follow him till the last drop of Abolition blood is shed ; or, led on in troops by such masters in infamy as Donaldson, Marshal of the United States, or Jones, the Sheriff of Douglas County, or David R. Atchison, who left his seat at Washington as President of the United States' Senate to engage in this unjust war, and under their generalship planting their cannon before the Free-state buildings in Lawrence, and reducing them to ashes, notwithstanding the unresisting surrender of the inhabitants.

It is of necessity impossible to estimate the number of this border-ruffian population, as the number itself varies with the political occasions which call them out.   In a single day of election, their number has been increased sometimes by the advent of at least 3,000, who have crossed the border in order to control the elections.   Many hundreds are at all times organized into volunteer companies, bearing such titles as " Kickapoo Rangers," " Platte County Rifles," " Shot-gun Militia."   In a circular issued by one of the Missouri societies a few weeks before my visit, the system is openly confessed, while they appeal for help to sustain more vigorously this organized border-ruffianism :—

" The western counties of Missouri have, for the last two years, been heavily taxed, both in money and time, in fighting the battles of the South. Lafayette county alone has expended more than $100,000 in money, and as much and more in time. Up to this time the border counties of Missouri have upheld and maintained the rights and interests of the South in this struggle, unassisted, and not unsuccessfully."

Not quite unassisted, either; for when I was in South Carolina, not long before, immense meetings were being held and large sums subscribed, in order, although far more than 1,000 miles removed, to express active sympathy with those who were fighting the pro-slavery battles in Kansas.

As these border-ruffians form a fluctuating population, so their mode of life and place of habitation are not those of permanent settlers. They collect mostly about the large hotels and groceries (which is the American emendation of the word " groggery") and bar-rooms and gambling-houses, where they remain " loafing about," as an American would term it, during the day, and at night throw themselves on the floor, if beds be scarce, their revolvers at their side, and thus, a dozen in a row, prepare themselves for next day's action.

The name border-ruffian is one they glory in. "I am a border-ruffian, I am; none of your city-raised Down-easters. I can draw my bead at forty rod, and bound to shoot centre, anyhow. If the crowd wish, I don't care if we have a hand-fight before this here bar. I'm dreadful easy to whip; yes, sir-ee, dreadful easy. So jest jump me up, stranger, and we'll smash in all-createdly." This, stripped of its many oaths, is a specimen of the ordinary way in which a border-man introduces himself. I have seen instances in which the name of " border-ruffian" has been given to a steamboat, or to a favourite horse or dog, or as a sign for a grocery. A peculiar style of hat enjoys the same very popular appellation. And the story is told—I know not with what truth—of one of the Missouri fair at a Kansas ball declining the hand of a Free-soiler on the ground that " she was a border-ruffian, and could not be seen dancing with an Abolitionist." There is romance, therefore, even in ruffianism.

Quitting, however, the chivalry of the South, the Free-state party claim notice. There are among these, as in the Southern party, the noisy as well as the quiet—those that take pleasure in political strife as well as those whose object is honest, peaceful settling. On the side of freedom there has been a needless amount of speech-making, and committee-forming, and resolution-passing, and pen-and-ink indignation, as well as more active efforts in the way of fortifying and trenching their stronghold, Lawrence, and organizing into volunteer armed corps. There has also been scrip issued and credit taken on the strength of the hoped-for Free-state of Kansas. But, injudicious as many of the acts of the Free-soil party may have been, they are at least free from the graver charge of unrestrained violence and lawlessness, of which the Southern party have given so many grievous exhibitions.

In General Lane the adherents of the Free-state cause have as a leader a man of spirit and determination, not numbering more than thirty-four years, but who, ten years ago, won laurels in the war with Mexico, and has since distin-

guished himself in a political career as Lieutenant-Governor of his native State, Indiana, and
latterly as a member of Congress.   The fiery
energy of Lane is counterbalanced by the cooler
temperament of the other most noted leader of
the Free-state forces, as well as Governor
under the Free-state constitution, General Robinson.   Robinson is by some years Lane's senior,
but is probably not more than forty years old,
although his careworn looks might betoken a
greater age.   By profession he is a physician.
He, too, has seen rough service in the field, can
tell of hair-breadth escapes, and has had some
experience in politics in the Legislature of
California.   He was returned to the Californian
Legislature, from the district of Sacramento,
whilst yet a prisoner on account of the part he
took in the disturbances which occurred there
in 1850, and in which he espoused the cause of
the squatters.   He was at the same time
wounded, to all appearance mortally.   He
recovered, however, from his wounds, was
acquitted from the charges of murder and conspiracy, under which he was arraigned, and
took his seat in the State Legislature.   During

the same year he was wrecked on his passage
to New York by way of Panama.* Governor
Robinson's chief value as a leader consists
in those qualities of caution, foresight and judgment, which, added to determined energy,
make a man wise to deliberate and bold to
act.   These rare qualities he has combined in
a remarkable manner. As a man of cool, deliberate action and never-failing resoluteness

---

* A few days after the above references to Dr. Robinson's
eventful experiences in California were written, our public
journals contained an account extracted from *El Nicaraguense*,
of the execution of Lieutenant Jennings Estelle in the city of
Granada, for the murder of his fellow-officer, Lieutenant
Charles Gordon.   As the name of Charles Robinson occurs in
the declarations committed to writing by Estelle shortly before
his execution, it may be interesting to extract a few lines of
the confession, as little doubt can exist that the " Charles Robinson" referred to is the later Governor Robinson of Kansas.
The following are Estelle's words :—

"I was born in Marshall, Tennessee, in the year 1833, and
was raised from my infancy in Hinds County, Mississippi.   I
started to California in 1852.   On the road I had a difficulty
with a man of the name of Howard, and shot him.   I afterwards shot a man of the name of Hays, but the wound did not
happen to prove fatal.   In the same year I had a difficulty
with Charles Robinson, and stabbed him in three places.   My
last two difficulties, while in California, occurred at the State
Prison, where I had been employed for the last two years.
After getting in the last scrape, I came to Nicaragua, and shot
Thomas Edwards.   I afterwards shot Charles Gordon."

of character, Governor Robinson has been in-
valuable to his cause, and has won the admiration of the opposite party. To such an extent
has the value of his services unfortunately been
recognized, that the party in power thought it
expedient to place their hands upon him and
detain him all the summer months of 1856 as
a prisoner, although untried and uncondemned.
The enormities of Naples and Austria are
reproduced in the United States of America.

In point of number the Free-state cause is
more largely represented in Kansas, I have
good ground for concluding, that the cause of
the South. In the election with a view to a
State constitution which took place on October
9, 1855, 2,710 Free-state men voted. In the
election of the Free-state candidate, Ex-Governor Reeder, as a delegate to Congress, 2,849
votes were cast. Allowing for an increase of
population during the succeeding year, and
making the necessary addition for the wives
and families of the voters, I have no doubt that
these figures will give a tolerably near approxi-
mation to the Free-soil population of Kansas.

That a Northern should flow in more readily

and more numerously than a Southern population is what might naturally be anticipated.
To the Northern man it is a small matter to
migrate towards the West in search of broader
lands and richer harvests.   To the Southern
planter it involves the removal of his stock of
slaves and the introduction of a system most
ill-adapted to the necessities of first settlement.
As a practical result, we have but to cast our
eye over the Western States and territories belonging to the North of the Union, and we see
a constant stream of immigration, so that fifty
waggons will sometimes be ferried across the
Mississippi in a single day, conveying in motley
grouping the earthly all of Eastern families
who have traversed probably a thousand or fifteen hundred miles to seek a new home in the
West.   It is estimated, indeed, that in the
Northern States there is an annual westward
flow of between 200,000 and 300,000 souls.   In
the South, on the other hand, the Western
migration advances with the slow steps which
attend the removal of a cumbersome machinery.

While, however, the Northern man has the
advantage in the facility of transit, and in that

instinct which impels the true Northerner, if he
do not succeed in one place, to seek better fortune in another, the inhabitant of the South,
and especially of the State of Missouri, has a compensation in the nearness of Kansas to his own
home, and the consequent ease with which he
can remove thither. We should anticipate, as
a result, that the Free States of the North
should give Kansas the larger number of its
permanent settlers, who have not journeyed
500, or 1,000, or 1,500 miles, simply to retrace
their steps; and that the Southern Slave States
would furnish the majority, if not the whole,
of its merely fluctuating and non-resident population. And so it is. Of its peaceable, industrious, order-loving population, nearly all are
true to the cause of liberty. This was not
only my own conclusion after coming in contact
with the settlers very generally, but was confirmed to me by the observation of one whose
opinion is entitled to the highest respect, and
whose official position must have enabled him
to form a very sound judgment upon the subject. This gentleman stated to me without
any hesitation, that "were the will of the ma-

jority of the Kansas settlers to determine, as the Organic Act prescribes, the territory's admission as a Free or Slave State, the question would, beyond a doubt, be decided in favour of freedom." My informant added the mournful remark, that he saw no near prospect of such a result, however much it was the will of the majority of those who had a right to will in the matter.

What the Free-state men have done in Kansas may be seen by a glance at their well-ordered " claims," or at Lawrence, Topeka, Pawnee, Osawatomie, Tecumseh, Council City, and the other places to which they have given an existence and a name. Lawrence is dignified with the name of city, and with its earth-works and circular forts intended to ward off a Proslavery attack, and its broad " Massachusetts street" occupied by stores and offices of greater and less architectural pretence, it is, for a Far-Western town, no inconsiderable place. The new Free-state Hotel, which was battered down with the aid of United States' cannon, was a substantial building of three stories, by far the finest as well as largest house in the whole territory. For the rest, Western cities must not be judged by European rules. They are always more remarkable on paper than in reality; and, whatever they can show in existence, they have much more in prospect. Still, the Free-State settlers in Kansas have, by the introduction of capital, given a more than usual impulse to settlement in that territory, and the steam saw-mill, the school-house, and the church attest the enterprise and the intelligence with which they have commenced their labours. Contrasting the towns built by the Free-state population with Leavenworth or other places where the majority are from the South, one remarks in the former a greater number of mechanics, shopkeepers, useful artisans, farmers, and rough labourers; and in the latter an excess of lawyers, doctors, land-speculators, rum-sellers, and bar-keepers.

Leavenworth City, and the manner of life in Kansas, both in town and country, I must reserve for another chapter.

CHAPTER XII.

Subject of the following Chapters.—Leavenworth City.—Far
Western Life.—Its accidental Features.—Fort Leavenworth.
—Appearance of the City.—Buildings.—Plan of the City.—
Remains of the primeval Forest.—Situation of the Houses.
—Laying out a City.—Most desirable Locations.—Increased
Value of Property.—Rapid Rise of a City.—Substantial
Buildings.—Wooden Shanties.

IN the following chapters I propose concluding
my description of life in Kansas by drawing in
outline a portraiture of Leavenworth City, as
the most populous and important place the
Southern men have had any hand in building;
and by glancing, in illustration of life in the
country, at the system pursued of entering,
claiming, clearing, log-hut erecting, and generally improving the land.

While, however, Leavenworth is the best
example of what a Southern population has
done in Kansas, I must in justice premise that
any rudeness which may be discovered in it
must not be wholly attributed to Southern

barbarity, but belongs rather to the essence of Far Western life. I only describe Leavenworth and the external appearance of Kansas Territory generally, with a view to enable those who are interested in the great struggle now taking place on that soil, to bring before their minds more vividly and truly the scenes and localities in the midst of which these important political events are occurring. I have withheld in these pages a description of much that is rough and uncivilized, lest a false argument should thence be constructed. There are many discomforts and many dangers on the border land which it were very unfair to associate with the perils arising from the revolvers of the "Regulators." In ascending the Missouri, for example, the steamboat was twice during the passage discovered to be on fire at a tender point near the furnaces; five or six times, also, it ran upon sandbanks, and had to be lifted off by a curious machinery of spars and derricks, by means of which the vessel is raised and made to walk over the bank, like some long-legged leviathan. Yet, in narrating the events which occurred on board, I felt bound to omit all notice of such accidental circumstances, lest they should unfairly be put to the charge of the border-ruffian company which it was my particular object to describe. They have enough that is bad to bear on their own account, without being made responsible for those other irregularities which universally, and as if by nature, characterize the rude life of the border.

"The finest city on the Missouri, heaps of stone buildings—quite a place," was the description given me of Leavenworth, shortly before reaching it, by my friendly adviser, the Indian trader of Easton. Too flattering an expectation only led to disappointment when I was put ashore among the rough log tenements which constitute the most prominent features of this embryo city. Three or four miles above, stands Fort Leavenworth, the chief garrison in the Territory, and the *entrepôt* for the supply of the forts beyond, as well as the place of departure for the Government trains. It stands upon a boldly-projecting bluff, far elevated above the Missouri, which rolls turbulently past its base, and, commanding a widely extending

view of the broad prairie ground towards the
west, its white walls and well-known flagstaff
form a most welcome signal of approaching
home to the traveller returning from the
plains.

A spot where the banks of the Missouri are
less elevated and abrupt has been wisely chosen
for the site of the city of Leavenworth.   Landing from the river, there is first a broad *levée* of
about half a mile, with a frontage of stores and
warehouses full of bustle and activity.   The
levée is the natural river bank, in the wet season
muddy, in the dry season parched and dusty,
against the steep acclivity of which the steamboat is thrust to discharge itself of its freight
and passengers.   The quay is broad, being
designed to receive all the business of the place
and of the country behind, which receives its
supplies through Leavenworth.   At the time
of my visit, goods of every kind lay in piles
upon the quay, while the road was further
blocked up with long waggons, each with six
or more yoke of oxen, preparing to cross the
plains.   The stores fronting the *levée* presented
an irregular line of erections, for the most part

built of wood; some of one story, some of two, but in all cases covered almost from top to bottom with signboards, inscribed in characters more remarkable for size than beauty. Passing back from the front street, other streets parallel and rectangular are reached, very regular as to their latitude and longitude, but very irregular in their grading. The city spreads over, in fact, an irregular space of about a square mile, the surface of the ground being exceedingly uneven, and occupied with buildings before it has received the needed levelling.

As in most Far Western towns, the houses are scattered over the place in detached erections at considerable intervals, with out-houses, commonly at a distance behind each. Could the plan of the city be carried in mental vision, the houses would be found to be very regularly built upon broad avenues, which, upon paper, make Leavenworth an imposing city. But as the trees of the primeval forest are not wholly removed, and their stumps continue to interrupt the intended thoroughfares, it is impossible at times to keep to the authorized avenue or street. The old pathway through the wood is

still most naturally followed, and, with nothing
to prevent the most direct route being taken,
the pedestrian finds himself following a track
which conducts him now along the line of a
future avenue, now diagonally intersecting it,
again branching off through a projected "im
provement," and then crossing what is one day
probably to be a garden, between some log-hut
and its yet humbler out-house.

The houses are widely scattered over the
ground, according to a custom in all Western
towns, which originates, doubtless, in the high
price charged for land. As soon as a spot is
recognized as a site of future greatness, the
land, which has been sold probably before for
one or two dollars per acre, rises, it may be, to
50 or 100 dollars. Land surveyors draw elabo-
rate plans. Streets are laid off, as rectangular
and equidistant as geometer could desire.
Broadway and Washington, Jefferson and Madison Avenues immediately take up the lati-
tudes; First, Second, Third, and Fourth Streets
are assigned the longitudes. As yet, probably,
not a tree has fallen before the axe. Town lots,
however, are sold to persons living at a dis-

tance. Lawyers help the surveyors, and surveyors help the lawyers, while both together
help the speculators. "Most desirable locations" meet speedy purchasers, who judge of
the value of their purchases from the map.
The few first settlers enter on their claims.
"Improvements" begin; the trees fall; the
prices rise; the speculators, the surveyors, and
the lawyers have all got well paid, and, in the
following year, by a process of which we might
question the straightforwardness, a whole city
has come into being, and all the representations
and promises of the map, so false in themselves,
have become actually realized. The consequence is that, in the city which, a twelvemonth before, was occupied only by the
Indian's wigwam, property has already acquired a high value, and every one is profiting
by a rising market. If the game is played
too hard by the speculators, a reaction will
sometimes ensue, and the settler suffers a
loss. But ordinarily he is no exception to
the general gain; for, although all the profits
realized are at his expense, the value of land
thus entered upon and constituted into a little

centre of commerce is sufficiently great to leave him in possession of a profitable investment. Singular as it may appear to us, this is the history of nearly all the towns and villages which, by the hundred, rise up yearly through the west of America ; and the high price which is put by anticipation upon the land is a sufficient reason why, in Leavenworth, as elsewhere, the settlers have preferred to get cheaper sites by spreading to a distance from the centre of business.

Some few of the buildings in Leavenworth are substantial stone erections of fair exterior, and a hotel on a large scale is projected ; but for the most part the houses are confined to the wooden shanty or the plain rough log-hut. The latter, however, belongs more to country than to city life, and is only to be seen in all its rude simplicity upon the " claim," where the settler is turning the bush into cultivated and productive farm land.

CHAPTER XIII.

Kansas Interiors.—The Log-hut.—Discomforts.—Wind and
Mud.—Strange Medley.—Various Modes of Construction.—
Different Stages of Log-hut building.—The Wooden House
and Shanty.—How it is built.—Tent-life.—Interior Economy.
—"Temperance House."—The Company.—Occupations.—
Unreasonable Demands for Accommodation.—Alligators
turned out.—Travel teaches Contentment.—Disallowed at
Night, but enforced by Day.—Conveniences of the Toilet.—
Meals.—Pride of the Host.—Rapid Eating.—Population of
Leavenworth.—Commerce of the Plains.—Value of Stock.—
Caravan Trains.

A DESCRIPTION of the home-life of Kansas
must commence with the log-hut as the most
elementary form of dwelling.

The external form of the log-hut is probably
familiar to most readers. But it would be difficult to convey to those accustomed to the
homes of England an idea of the dirt, discomfort, and misery which often reign within. In
justice I must add that I have seen remarkable
exceptions to this — especially in the backwoods
of Canada and of the North Western States of

the Union. The Western border-man, however, loves his rude cabin with all its apparent
discomforts. The wind which enters in gusts
through the broad gaping chinks betwixt log
and log is to him an agreeable ventilation;
wanting this, the place would feel close and
remind him of the pitiable habitations of " city-
raised Down-Easters." The filth upon the
floor, the smoke which fills the air, the blend-
ing of diverse odours arising from the cooking
of hog-flesh over the fire and the presence of
the living hog-flesh in the room, the interming-
ling of pig and poultry, parent and child, within
the same few yards square, the strange decking
of sides and roof with household stores and
buffalo-skins, rifles, hatchets and powder-horns,
all these things seem to be elements of charmed
life to the true-born Western man.

There are stages of progress, too, in log-hut
building. The most elementary is that in which
the logs are piled one above another in a single
square, notched and saddled so as to fit into one
another angularly at about a foot short of the
extremity of each log, and thus to form a stout
framework, sawn through at the place where

the door is intended, and the whole capped by
a roofing of timber covered with broad flat
pieces of wood, called "shakes." If the settler
desires to have his cabin plastered, he uses mud.
Within, for furniture, he contents himself with
a few tree-stumps, nicely trimmed, for seats,
and a shelf or two, to do service in place of
bedsteads. In dry weather the cooking is most
conveniently managed outside the dwelling.
This is the first stage of log-hut building. The
second is marked by the introduction of the
chimney. This is commonly built outside the
house, as an adjunct; or rather, one might say,
the house seems to be built against the chimney,
so speedily has that which is but a novel inven-
tion come to be regarded, if one may judge from
its size and prominence, as the most important
feature. The third stage — if one may pass
over the introduction of a second floor, reached
by a rough ladder of home manufacture — is
that in which further accommodation is sought
laterally. This is accomplished by building a
second square hut at, probably, twelve feet distance from the first and carrying the roof across
the intervening space, so that a single house is

formed, consisting of rooms right and left, and an open reception-room in the centre, where meals can be taken if desired, free to the air at its two sides, but shielded above by the roof covering. This is the highest style of log-house, and one much in favour in some parts of the Far West.

For the city life of Leavenworth, however, the log-hut is naturally discarded for the more polished shanty, or the yet larger wooden house. Sawn timber costs less in many parts of Kansas than the rough log, the groves and forests being far from plentiful, even in the east of the territory. A frame is run up and the planks nailed together, much as in any other place, understanding always that the rough settler is not particular about the right relation of the door to the doorway, or the nice fitting together of the plank sides, or the general finish and architectural correctness of either exterior or interior. That, when built, it is next furnished can scarcely be said of one of these Western houses. The settler commonly arrives at the place of his choice, strikes his tent, deposits his household furnishings and implements of husbandry

and war, and it then remains to build his house
around his furniture rather than to introduce
his furniture into his house.   I have seen many
instances in which a family has been living
half within and half without their house, their
domestic arrangements being in a state of
incompleteness.   On the very outskirts, too,
of Leavenworth, I have remarked families
living, Indian-like, beneath a rude covering
of branches and mud, or under a simple awning
stretched across a pole, amid the thick brush-
wood which skirts the steep banks of the Missouri.   In the city itself, however, there are
many houses of two stories, and comparative
comfort, such as would be called in the vernac-
ular of the West "mighty fine," "elegant,"
"right smart," "all-fired grand and Down-East
like."

As an illustration of the interior economy
of one of these better houses, I will attempt
a brief sketch of that which was my own home
while in Leavenworth City.   "Temperance
House" was a newly erected, low-roofed,
wooden building, with two rooms in front,
and others at the rear.   The name was an

attraction to me, from the certainty that the worst of the Missourian borderers would most decidedly eschew a house where the bar-room was destitute of " liquor." I had reason to be satisfied with it, for the company was the quietest and most sober I saw in Leavenworth, and permitted me to stay there without the customary inquiry " whether I was sound on the goose." They were evidently for the most part Free-state men, although in their constant political discussions none ventured to make the admission. The house was approached by a narrow gallery, with steps at each end, always occupied by a row of men who sat, some on the gallery rail, others on chairs tilted against the house, others with their feet upon the rail-top. Their employment was to chew, to spit, to talk politics, and to whittle. From the gallery were entered the two front rooms. That on the left was the bar-room, with nothing stronger wherewith to satisfy thirst than a bucket of water and a tin dipper, placed upon the counter; and beyond it the dining-room and other apartments. That on the right was my own bedroom.

There was a certain air of cleanliness and of

the intention of comfort about the place which bespoke it the work of a Northern man. Most generously, too, the host granted me exclusive right and privilege in relation to the front sleeping apartment, which he " allowed to believe was the finest room in the house." This concession was not made, it is true, without the exercise of some tact and persuasion. The room contained, unfortunately, two large beds. Mine host " calculated the stranger could not want more than one, *at most*." There were several, he said, occupying the room at the time. Beds were scarce in Leavenworth. I had myself been offered at the two principal hotels nothing better than " a chance on the floor." My request for the whole room, with its accommodation for at the least four persons, was evidently highly unreasonable, and as unaccountable as it was unreasonable. I explained, however, that I had a singular love for privacy at night, albeit he would not find me unsociable as a guest by day. I gave him to understand, also, that the indulgence of my peculiarity of taste was the condition of my staying in his house, but that he would not find me indisposed to meet any just claim he might have upon me in consequence. Mine host was conquered. He engaged to do what he could to accommodate the occupants of the room elsewhere, with much consideration adding, " If any of the alligators come in, just make them put, Colonel." I promised, and acted upon my promise.

When I returned to my room at night, I had opportunity to examine it at leisure. Looked at with Eastern eyes, it was open to unfavourable criticism. The apartment itself was rude and cheerless; its sides of rough, unpainted deal were not proof against the entrance of draughts, and permitted communication with adjoining rooms by either sound or sight; its floor was, of course, uncarpeted; its two beds offered nothing better than shuck mattresses and dirty blankets; washing-stands and looking-glasses were out of the question; three or four chairs and a small rickety table formed the only additional furniture. Nevertheless, travel in the West soon teaches one that, if the essentials are present, it is a folly to distress oneself about minor accessories. I was not long in discovering that a mattress, though made of the crackling leaves of the Indian corn, is welcome to weary bones, and that the draughts of air which passed through the open chinks were more than compensated by the relief they afforded from the suffocating heat. Locks and bolts had not yet been introduced for use on the door. The door opened upon the street, and in that street were collected some of the basest ruffians that ever disgraced humanity. But an adjustment of a chair against the door caused an alarm with every incursion, and, as very fortunately the most violent did not intrude, a discreet assertion of my prerogative in relation to both beds was sufficient to preserve the privacy of my room. Not so, however, during the day; but, knowing that to the Western man a refusal is an incomprehensible selfishness, I made, for the sake of peace and goodwill, a free surrender throughout the day of the room, with its beds, chairs, table, and floor, all of which were as freely used, that I might have the better claim for indulgence at night. The conveniences of the toilette were wanting, but, as in all Far Western places, there was a board behind the house on which stood a couple of tin basins filled with the muddy water of the Missouri, while a square foot of mirror, with brush and comb attached by means of a string, hung upon the wall for the use of " the crowd." In all this there was evident intention to provide for the necessities of the guests, and I very heartily thanked the worthy host for setting so good an example of hotel keeping in Kansas.

The host particularly prided himself on the powers of his cook, and the superiority of his table generally. " Step in, stranger; the crowd's going in to eat," was my summons, soon after six o'clock, to breakfast; the same at half-past twelve for dinner; and at six in the evening for supper. These are the good hours kept generally by Western folk. I entered the dining-room, saw the table covered with breakfast fare, including the usual small dishes of meat and cakes and apple preserve. The " crowd" was standing around the table, each man with a hand upon the back of his chair. The female portion of the company having been seated, a signal was given, and a

simultaneous action ensued. The movement
of the chair with one hand, the seizure of
the nearest small dish with the other, the
sudden sitting down, and the commencement
of a vigorous eating, were the work of a
moment. In five minutes the company had
left the table for the gallery on the street front,
the better for damper, Indian-corn bread eaten
with molasses, sliced bacon cooked, apparently,
in grease, and tea or coffee. Some few, more
fortunate or more quick to seize opportunities,
had obtained a piece of Johnny-cake, or some
apple-sauce, or other delicacy from the smaller
dishes, in addition. At dinner it was the same
—fat bacon, corn-bread, and tea or coffee. At
supper, the same ; and at each meal in about
equal quantity. The next day the same, and so
every day. I concluded, in relation to the
whole subject of the domestic economy of
Kansas, that unsophisticated nature is contented
with little, and that in Kansas, nature is allowed
to have very much her own way in this particular.

The population of Leavenworth City fluctu-
ates much with political occasions. It would

be safe to estimate it, however, at about 1,500. I speak of the time of my visit, when it had been little more than eighteen months in existence as a settlement. It owes its prosperity, in great part, to its favourable position on the Missouri, which brings to it much of the great commerce of the plains and the traffic with the Indians, in addition to the home trade of the territory. The commerce of the plains, which, during more than thirty years, has been rising in importance, has become, since the war with New Mexico, and the removal of commercial restrictions which has followed the war, a most valuable feature in the Kansas trade. Setting aside the very numerous trains in the service of the Government, which maintain communication between Fort Leavenworth and the outposts on the Santa Fé and Oregon routes, the annual value of the regular commerce amounts to from $2,000,000 to $3,000,000. This employs many hundreds of waggons, and a still larger number of men, and tends materially to keep up the price of labour in the territory. Each waggon, again, requires twelve or more oxen, and a great number of mules are also employed on the expeditions. This makes the rearing of stock a very profitable employment for the farm lands in Kansas and Missouri. The trains go almost exclusively during the spring and summer months, when the prairie grass furnishes the necessary food for the animals. According to the season, they get over from ten to twenty miles in the day. A waggon is estimated to carry about 5,500 lb. The expense of transport varies with the season. It ranges from a little over $1 in the best months to as much over $2 in the worst months, per hundred-weight per 100 miles. The distance from Leavenworth to Santa Fé is between 800 and 900 miles. In the winter months, when the journey is accompanied by great hardship and peril, the mail is the only communication, which is transported once a month by means of mules. With Oregon the trade on the plains has almost ceased in favour of the route by the Pacific; but the Government has still occasion to use the Oregon track as far as Fort Kearney and Fort Laramie, a distance of 600 miles. The great traffic, however, is to Fort Riley, Fort Munn, and thus to Santa Fé. Independence in Mis-

souri, Kansas City on the border, and Leavenworth, are all made use of as the *entrepôts*
of this trade ; and few things can be imagined
more strangely picturesque than the sight
which these cities present when, in the spring
or early summer, their streets are filled with
scores of long, cumbrous-looking covered waggons, and hundreds of oxen and mules ; while a
noisy crew of light-hearted adventurers—Missourian, Spanish, half-breed, and Indian—dressed in every variety of romantic costume, are
busied in fitting out their train for its many
weeks' journeying over the rolling grassy plains
of the Western prairies.

CHAPTER XIV.

Traffic with the Indians.—How it is carried on.—Business and
Pleasure.—Good Per-centage.—Busy Appearance of Leavenworth.—Necessaries of civilized Life.—Steamboats.—Railroads.—The Electric Telegraph.—Squatter-life.—Land without a Title.—The "Claim."—Division of new Lands.—A
"Bee."—"Log-rolling."—Squatter Sovereignty.—"Tomahawk Rights."—"Entering," or "Pre-empting."—Abuses
of the System.—"Jumping."—"Foundations."—A "Caution."—Right of Suffrage.

An important item in the commerce of Leavenworth is that which is brought to it by the
Red Rovers of the prairie.

The traffic with the Indians is a feature by
itself, and one of not inconsiderable importance,
in the trade of Kansas. It rests almost exclusively, however, in the hands of one òr two
parties, who, having been known by the Indian
tribes for years, are able to monopolize the
trade. The chief mode of carrying it on is
the following :

Every quarter of a year the Indian tribes to

which allowances are due receive their payment from the Government agent.   On the day of payment a grand feast is prepared by the merchant, and notice is sent to the various Indian tribes of the hospitalities to which they are invited.   The entertainment is often very costly; the more costly the more profitable. On quarter's day the Indians come down, after long journeying, men, women, and children, often to the number of three or four hundred, to receive their pay and to make their purchases of white men's manufacture.   With their pockets full, they sit down to the feast; eat, drink, and are merry ; at the same time are forgetful ordinarily of the rules of prudence.   The result is a large sale, and the next day the tribes are seen returning, the men with their hatchets and knives and accoutrements of all sorts ; and the squaws with their shawls and blankets, and beads and trinkets, often to the value of thou sands of dollars.   One Indian trader sells annually about $10,000.   At a recent sale the amount expended by the Indians reached $3,000.   The account might be analyzed as follows :

		Dollars.
Cost price of articles . . .		1,000
Expenditure on feast . . .		500
Balance of profit cleared . .		1,500

3,000

Many of the articles yield 200 per cent.
profit; but 150 per cent. is probably a fair
average. In the traffic with the Indians generally there are more tact and shrewdness manifested by the traders than fair dealing. In fact,
honour, honesty, morality, all that is good, is
lamentably rare in the Western border-land.
The frontiersman has a manliness and generosity
of his own which all must admire, but these
qualities spring from the peculiarities of his
position on the outskirts of civilization. There
is little, it is to be feared, of higher motive.
For the rest, the Western borderer is almost as
untutored as a savage. He thinks little about
his maker, God; as a consequence it comes, also,
that he thinks and cares little about his fellow-
man.

With a commerce thus extended, the quays

of Leavenworth present a busy appearance, and had not peaceful industry been diverted by the turbulence of evil passions into other channels, the newly-settled Territory would have been blessed already with a large measure of prosperity. As it is, large steamers daily pass up and down, and find active employment in the transport of goods and passengers. The imports of manufactured goods are very large ; and, while some of what we should deem the necessaries of civilized life are but beginning to be introduced, I have observed, as a contrast, one or two piano-fortes being landed, to supply the wants, no doubt, of some refined denizen of the Eastern States.

The size and number of the steamboats on the Missouri would occasion surprise to one unaccustomed to the rapid progress the Western world exhibits in all that furthers the building up of cities and the extension of commerce. I counted upon its waters from ten to fifteen large steamboats, each capable of accommodating, on the average, a hundred passengers at the least, and in effect carrying many more, in addition to their cargo, besides a much larger number of steamers of less capacity; all of which were regularly employed upon the trade of the Missouri. This large traffic is in great part sustained by Kansas. Yet eighteen months before, there was not so much as a village of white settlers within the whole extent of the Territory. Railroads are already projected, but how far their formation is to be looked for as a speedy occurrence is doubtful, because the bills which empowered their construction, and which passed the first Legislature, were evidently a part of a false system of legislation, which grants the constitution of companies in order to gain the constituents as adherents and supporters of the granting power. The electric telegraph, however, is a mark of progress which, if not already, soon will be among the things accomplished. I remember observing the wires for several hundred miles up the Missouri, as far as Independence and Liberty, which are close to the Kansas border-line. In a very brief space of time they would, doubtless, be carried into the Territory.

It is rather remarkable that, so far as Leavenworth city is concerned, the " improvements,"

as all erections are called in America, are made
upon land the tenure of which is not yet ascertained to the holders. The truth is that
Leavenworth is built upon land still of right
belonging to the Delaware Indians, and for
which the price to be paid as purchase-money
is not yet determined.   It might occasion
wonder that men should be induced, without a
title to the soil, to expend the sums which have
been laid out on some of the more solid and
permanent buildings in the city.   Sales are already effected, and land stands at a high price in
the market for which the title does not yet exist,
except the title of long occupation, which
assigns it to the Delawares.   All these mys-
teries, however, become unravelled as the eye
is opened to the methods of dealing adopted by
our astute American cousins towards the Indian
race.   The day soon comes when the lots, on
which the city stands, are put up to auction
for the benefit of the old possessors of the soil.
Bidding takes place.   The price is perfectly
understood beforehand.   Occupant A bids his
price for his own lot, B for his ; A does not interfere with B, and B does not interfere with A.

Western honor forbids over-bidding, although the market value of the land may be ten times that offered. The auction terminates; the accounts are settled; the Indian must take his money, with the usual deductions, and go further West; and the President of the United States grants a title-deed in his own name to the preëmptor of the soil. Many in Leavenworth are only speculators, who have entered lots in the city in order to realize with the advancing value of land.

Passing from town to country, the squatter life of Kansas claims notice by peculiarities of its own, as well as those which it has in common with other Western territories. The log-hut, which I have already described, will furnish the reader with one important element in the life of the country. The log-hut stands in the midst of the " claim," generally of 160 acres, called a quarter-section; and there, on his own freehold, the settler copes with the first difficulties, and commonly also reaps the after-fruit which belongs to the pioneer in the wilderness. In Kansas, however, as indeed in a less degree in other newly-settled Western lands, this pro-

cedure is not marked by so much definiteness
and regularity as might at the first be supposed.
Even granting that all is previously arranged
with the Indians, the title cannot be given
until the Government-survey is made, which,
by an excellent system, divides all new lands
in the United States into counties, townships,
sections, and quarter-sections, of equal size and
perfect regularity of latitude and longitude.
But long before the survey is completed, the
squatter is upon the ground. He has already
paced out his 160 acres, or his 320 acres, or
whatever larger or smaller quantity of land he
wishes to possess. He has begun to clear. The
first trees he fells are already shaped into logs
for his hut; with smaller wood he is beginning
his fencing. He has summoned a "bee," and a
"log-rolling" has taken place; that is, he has
asked neighbouring settlers to lend him their aid
by rolling the logs to the site of his future
home—a service which they are at liberty to ask
of him in return when occasion requires. Lastly, the arrow is marked over his doorway, and
his name probably added besides, to warn all
after-comers to respect prior rights.

It is this system which constitutes "squat-ting." The land is free. The settler may choose his home wherever he may please, provided no one else is before him in the field. " Squatter sovereignty," and what are called " tomahawk rights," are introduced, and be-come the incipient law of the future territory. None durst interfere, if he might, with a "claim" thus made. The notice given to the Govern-ment authorities secures the pre-emption. The act itself is called that of " entering," or " pre-empting." When, probably a couple of years later, the survey is completed, and land-offices are opened in the territory, the squatter, if he chooses to retain the land, of which he has had the free use, offers at the land sale the upset price of $1¼ per acre, over which no one bids against him, and the land becomes his by legal right and title. During the first stage, mutual protection is given to the squatters by their forming into " Squatters' Associations;" and the " squatter-right" to a lot of ground is bought and sold on the strength of the law which ema-nates from these associations, and which asserts its power by rifle and tomahawk.

Such is squatting theoretically, and as practised in its purest forms,—a rough method, but
one well adapted for the country to which it is
applied. But there are many abuses to which
this system has become, in Kansas, at least,
subject in practice. Such an abuse is the
practice technically called "jumping a claim,"
—one which has been only too frequent in the
unsettled condition of the territory. To jump
a claim is to take it, notwithstanding that it is
pre-occupied by one who has already given
notice of his claim to a pre-emptive title. The
temptation to jump lies in the advantage of
entering into another man's labours, and becoming the happy possessor of improvements
without the necessity of toiling for them.
The price of jumping is ordinarily a fight.
There is no other way of settling such matters.
Neighbours, however, will generally help, being
guided by their political sentiments as to the
side they shall espouse. The weaker then
goes to the wall,—a result which many Free-
state settlers have had occasion to deplore in
the numerous instances in which the act of
jumping has been sustained by numbers and

combined strength beyond their power to resist. The fighting which follows has sometimes led to very serious consequences. More than one of the chief movements in the political history of Kansas have had their origin in difficulties arising from this prolific source. Even the House of Assembly has not been free from angry debates between members of the Legislature resulting from disputed claims. And one instance, at least, is known in the Upper House in which violent blows between the eyes, and other expressions of injured honour, were interchanged by two members of Council, in order to settle a difficulty originating in the precarious rights of Squatterdom.

There are other abuses to which the system is subject, which it is unnecessary to explain in detail; but it may not be uninteresting to advert to one development of Kansas squatting, which, to the eye of the traveller, appears singularly ridiculous. Often, in riding over the prairie, the traveller meets with a small clearance, sufficient, at least, to show that some one has been there. Then, probably, a few stakes are seen; the settler has evidently intended to

stake off his ground. Next appears the "foundation"—four logs, perhaps, placed in a quad-
rangle, the earnest, apparently, of the log-hut
that is to follow. And, on a bit of stick, lastly,
or on a piece of paper nailed to a tree, appear
the words, in a scarcely legible scrawl, " This
is Jim Barton's claim; and he'll shoot the
first fellow as comes within a mile of it." Such
an announcement is technically called a " caution." As you read, you instinctively draw
back; and, if on the look-out for a claim yourself, you seek fortune further on. But Jim
Barton's "foundation" will probably never be
occupied. If you are pleased with the site,
you may avail yourself of Mr. Barton's beginning, and little fear his caution. Most probably
that gentleman lives in a neighbouring State,
but desires the elective franchise in Kansas.
Anxious to give some colour to his claim as
a voter, he has set his mark on a piece of land,
and henceforth claims the privileges of an
owner of the soil. But this is against all squatting law and precedent, which requires that
every squatter personally reside upon his claim.
The men of Missouri, however, framed squatter

laws for themselves in relation to Kansas; among them, that "protection should be afforded to no Abolitionist settlers;" and, with the dangerous power conferred by recent legislation on "squatter sovereignty," they have found themselves free to exercise with impunity their own sovereign will.   Many affirmed their right to a vote in the territory, although they only threw down an axe upon the ground; others, if they only intended at some time to make a claim; others, again, if they were only on the ground on the day of election.

CHAPTER XV.

The Geography of Kansas.—Junction of the Kansas and Missouri Rivers.—Kansas City.—The Santa Fé Road.—Settlements up the Kansas River.—Lawrence.—Lecompton.—Topeka.—Kaw Half-breeds.—Fort Riley.—Mounds.—California Road.—The Oregon Trail.--Crossing the Plains.—Character of the Country.—The Great American Desert.—The Rocky Mountains.—Banks of the Missouri.—Leavenworth City and Fort.--Western Routes.—The Upper Missouri.--Osawatomie.—Climate and Soil of Kansas.—Production.--Wages.

A TRAVELLER, approaching Kansas from the East by way of the Missouri, first sees the territory at the point of confluence of the Missouri and Kansas Rivers. On his right, the Missouri, which at this point suddenly changes its course, pours down its muddy volume from the North, bringing the washings of thousands of miles, which render its waters at some seasons of the year so densely turbid, that an object cannot be seen if lying a few inches beneath the surface. On his left, flows into it a somewhat purer and less turbulent stream, the Kaw or Kansas River, which, intersecting the Territory which bears its name in a direction almost due West and East, leaves fertility all along its course, and from between thickly clustering oak and elm, maple and hickory, which beautifully shade its banks, terminates its windings in the rolling flood of the Missouri.

At the point of junction between the two rivers, the traveller will discern amongst the wood the little Indian village known as Wyandot city, planted on the reserve belonging to the pale-faced tribe, which Cooper has rendered famous by his novel of " Wyandotte." On the left, facing the Missouri, at a short distance below the junction, stands the bustling little town called Kansas city, where the traveller will probably be induced to land. If its crowded *levée* or quay were to be taken away, little would be left to Kansas city. It is oddly wedged in, like the lower town of Quebec in Canada, upon a narrow slip of land between the river and a steep bluff, so that if the city wish to extend its boundaries, it can only do so, as in the Canadian city, by mounting the bluff behind it, and forming an upper town.

From Kansas city the traveller may strike for the West, in order to form his first acquaintance with the territory. He may take the "Santa Fé Road," in which case he will enter Kansas, after passing Westport, at the Shawnee Manual Labour School. He will see the Rev. Thomas Johnson's farm, as well as the Baptist and the Friends' Mission. Forty miles will bring him to Hickory Point, after which he will, in a second or third day's journey, ride through Willow Springs to Hundred and Ten. Sixty miles more of rolling prairie and grassy plain will take him to Council Grove, or Big John Spring, where, as the name indicates, the traveller may hold his council, and determine whether, having followed the Santa Fé Road for a hundred and thirty miles, he will trust himself to the trail for a prairie-ride of weeks into the territory of New Mexico. This is the most Southern of the great routes. As far as Council Grove, it carries the traveller across an undulating tract, often over high wave-like ridges, commanding extensive views across the broad savannahs; and, before he has reached Hickory Point, the course of the streams, or creeks as they are there termed, will have indicated to the observer that he has left the valley of the Kaw, and that he is skirting the basin of the Osage and other large rivers of the South.

Or, from Kansas city, the traveller may take the more frequented "California Road," in order to trace upward the Kansas river, and see the towns and settlements which have risen so rapidly upon its banks. In this case he has a ride of about forty miles, passing through a woody tract of country belonging, by Govern-ment-grant, to the Shawnee Indians, until he reaches the shady banks of the Wakarusa. Crossing the creek, he sees the spot famous as the camping-ground of the Governor's troops during the siege of Lawrence; then, passing through Franklin, a strong pro-slavery village, he has four miles yet before him, and at length finds himself in the Free-state stronghold of Lawrence. Following for twelve miles more the southern margin of the Kaw, the traveller reaches Lecompton, the capital of the Terri-tory, according to the designation of the Terri-torial Legislature. The situation of Lecompton is less attractive than that Lawrence, but it has received some impulse by being made the seat of Government. The military tents are probably now removed, but there for long the soldiers' tents marked the site of the Western encampment, and the place of confinement for the Free-state Governor, editors, and a hundred more political offenders. Another twelve miles' stage takes the traveller through Tecumseh to Topeka, where he sees the little building known by the Free-state people as Constitution Hall, and finds himself at the seat of Government and intended capital under the Free-state *régime.*

Here our explorer will probably cross the river, and as he wanders about its northern bank, and passes from grove to thicket, and creek to prairie, he will see, here and there, a curling smoke, and, on nearer approach, will find, he is on a spot where a few families of Kaw half-breeds have erected their wigwams, and made for themselves a home. From the Indian village he may return, if he please, through the Delaware reserve to Kansas city; following in this case the left bank of the river, and coming out by the old Delaware road at Wyandot city, whence he reaches his destination, after a homeward journey of about seventy miles; or he may take the military road to Leavenworth, a distance of about fifty miles, passing on his way the Grasshopper and Stranger Creeks, and gently ascending or descending with the wavy roll of the prairie. It may be, however, that the traveller wishes to strike for the West, in which case he may follow upward the course of the Kansas River by the Fort Riley Road, passing the St. Mary's Catholic Mission, crossing the Vermilion and Big Blue Rivers, and glancing at a few small villages founded by Free-state settlers, until he reaches Pawnee and Fort Riley, at the confluence of the Smoky Hill and Republican Forks. At various points in the course of his journeying, the traveller will have observed mounds, apparently natural, but sometimes showing indications of artificial erections upon their summit, which will remind him of the interesting mounds in the Ohio and the Mississippi valleys, and suggest speculations as to the earlier dwellers upon the banks of the Kaw.

Should the inclinations of the traveller lead

him towards California, he has but to take the
California road branching out in a northwesterly
direction after crossing the Vermilion Creek, and
he will strike, in about forty miles, the great
Oregon and California trail, which, patiently
followed through a number of weary weeks,
will conduct him in safety to the golden State,
For the first thousand miles, as far as Bear
River, the Oregon, Californian, and Utah parties journey together, taking the North Fork
of the Platte River, and crossing the Rocky
Mountain chain by the great South pass. At
Bear River they part. The few who go to
Oregon have another thousand miles before
them. The Californians have an equal distance,
dropping their Mormon companions eighty
miles upon their route, as they pass the city of
the Great Salt Lake. According to the route
traversed, the entire length of the ride varies
from 2050 to 2350 miles. A like distance,
could it be laid off from London in a direct line,
would transport a person eastward to the borders of Tartary, or to the banks of the Tigris
and Euphrates; or southward, it would lead
him beyond the limits of the Great Desert of

Africa.   Yet, as many as eighty thousand travellers have been known to cross the plains in a single year.   It is unnecessary to remark that these overland expeditions, with the large waggons and long teams of oxen and innumerable mules which accompany them, imply a prairie traffic of not inconsiderable activity.

By all accounts, these long overland journeys, after the first novelty is passed, are far from attractive.   The slow ascent and descent of the prairie waves, the crossing of interminable savannahs, without an object, except the faithless mirage, to relieve the dead uniformity of the scene, the horizon of prairie-grass ever encircling the traveller, however interesting for the first day or two, become after a time unspeakably monotonous.   The flying of the eagle overhead, the starting of a herd of buffalo, the meeting of another train of travellers, the encounter of a party of Indians, friendly or hostile, come to be the notable events of the pilgrimage, even as, on an ocean voyage, the dull monotony is relieved by the sighting of a distant sail, the exchange of news with a returning ship, the disturbance of a shoal of sharks, or the catching of some luckless whale.

On the Westward route, moreover, the attractions of the landscape and the comforts of the traveller suffer a speedy decrease, while dangers multiply and miseries of every kind grow apace. For the first hundred and fifty miles the road traverses richly-wooded, rolling prairie, on which the fertile soil has caused so luxuriant a growth of prairie-grass, that the traveller may sit down and conceal himself in its midst. The fertile region of "tall grass" being left behind, broad, sandy plains are reached, almost destitute of timber, but carpeted with the fine, slender "buffalo-grass," which countless herds of buffalo, elk, and antelope keep short by their constant browzing. These pasture lands continue for about 350 miles westward. The rivers, which cut their deep channels through this region, afford the traveller only too frequent occasions for practice in the art of fording, which, with the scores of oxen and the long heavy waggons which accompany the caravan, is a process involving difficulty and frequent danger. The larger streams are crossed by boats.

At length the finely-cropped buffalo-grass disappears, and nothing is left but a sterile waste, of a light sandy color, unrelieved by river, rock, or tree. The soil is a kind of marl, with indications of limestone. This tract is known as the "Great American Desert," and stretches from North to South over 1,000 miles of country. In following the Santa Fé trail, wild, roving tribes of Cheyennes and Arapahoe Indians will probably be met in this district, as in the preceding the hunting-grounds of the Kaws are traversed. On the Oregon trail, the unfortunate traveller may cross the path of the savage Sioux, who, if they have come down from the North on an expedition of warfare or revenge, will not spare. The western boundary of the desert region exhibits a curious phenomenon. Here and there, and in some parts in considerable number, appear elevations of the soil, platforms rather than mounds, perpendicular at the side, and flat upon the surface, varying in height from fifteen to fifty feet, and of exceedingly various breadth. These flat mounds are commonly called *buttes*, a word adopted from the Canadian French. The

Spaniards of New Mexico call them *cerros*. Through the action of the weather, these *buttes* assume frequently most fantastic shapes, reminding one of gaunt battlements and towers. Hence the well-known Court House, Cathedral, and Chimneys, familiar to the traveller on the Oregon trail.

From this point to the Rocky Mountains, the country is represented by travellers in glowing colours. They speak of a rich soil, of fertilizing streams, of well-timbered groves, of a genial climate, of attractive landscape, of sunny slopes and sheltered valleys, of laughing waterfalls, and green quiet meadow-lands, of fruits for every taste, and flowers of every hue. Whether an actual paradise or not, these pleasant characteristics seem to belong to the slopes and spurs of the Rocky Mountains throughout the Southern portion of the chain.

I have thus far attempted to describe the geographical features of Kansas, as seen by the traveller who ventures across the plains, gathering my information from the narratives of the expeditions of Colonel Fremont, Colonel Emory, and other explorers. I must again return to ground trodden by myself.

I have already accompanied the traveller from Kansas city up the Kaw River to the various settlements upon its banks. It remains that that portion of Kansas be visited, which lies upon the Missouri bank, and confronts the counties of Clay, Jackson, and Platte, in Missouri State.

In ascending the Missouri, the thirty miles which intervene between Kansas city and Leavenworth, present little to detain the traveller. Both in Kansas on his left, and Missouri on his right, he sees a rich reddish soil of great depth, inviting to the agriculturist and the raiser of stock, and giving promise of speedily yielding support to a busy population. Delaware city is passed,—a small cluster of houses, which would probably not have attained civic honours, were it not for the sanguine aspirations of land-speculators. Within a few miles is the Moravian Mission to the Munsees,—a mere fragment of that tribe, who, with a few families of Stockbridge Indians, do not number more than about a hundred and fifty souls. Then come Leavenworth city and Fort Leavenworth, of which some description has been already attempted.

From the Fort, should the traveller desire to explore the interior, he has choice of two roads, both leading Westward. The more Southern one, called the Fort Riley Road, passes through Easton, and strikes the Kaw nearly opposite Topeka. The more Northern, likewise a Government road, takes to Fort Kearney, where it joins the great trail up the valley of the Platte, and conducts, by the route already described, to the South Pass, and thence to the Pacific Ocean.

Ascending the Missouri from Leavenworth, Kickapoo is speedily reached, after which Weston is seen on the Missouri side. At thirty miles distance is Atchison, the home of Dr. Stringfellow, and the town whence his furious *Squatter Sovereign* is issued. Doniphan, Lewiston, Palermo—small places chiefly settled from Missouri—succeed; and then, sixty miles above Leavenworth, the steamboat reaches ordinarily its last landing-place at St. Joseph's—popularly called St. Joe's—in Missouri. Some steamers ascend the river higher to Nebraska, in which case they make Council Bluffs, 270 miles above Leavenworth, their final destination, embarking or disembarking at that point those passengers who reach the Territory by the Northern route through Iowa.

Having reached the end of population Northward, it remains only to say that there are one or two roads Southward from Kansas city, which conduct to the Osage River, besides the Sac trail which leads from the Santa Fé road to the Neosho or Grand River. Upon the Osage, near the junction of the Pottawatomie, is a Free-state settlement, which, very much in defiance of sound philology, has been named Osawatomie, the design being to preserve in the name of the town some respectful remembrance of the two streams, by the side of which it is built. Unphilosophical, however, as such a system of nomenclature may be, it has a better claim to originality than that exhibited in a small town in the extreme North, for which the fertile brains of the inhabitants could invent no better name than Lawrence No. 2.

The climate and soil of Eastern Kansas offer much that is inviting to the settler. The extremes of heat and cold in the summer and winter seasons are indeed much in excess of anything experienced in England. Nevertheless, the temperature is more moderate than in many parts of the American continent, and the Territory is situated within that favoured zone which makes it rich as a corn and hemp producing country. The crop of Indian corn, as far as I could ascertain, has generally yielded from fifty to eighty bushels per acre. Wheat, fifteen to twenty bushels. Hemp, which on the Missourian side of the river is the chief staple, is there found to yield in favourable situations 1,000 lbs. to the acre. Tobacco may probably be grown in some portions of the Territory.

The wages paid for farm labour at the time of my visit, were about the same as those paid for white labour in Missouri. Men employed in sawing and clearing—the principal work of the Western settler—obtained twenty dollars per month and their board. But a fine field for the intelligent and enterprising is offered by the overland trains, which give employment at high wages to a large number of the younger men. In some instances I learned that superior hands were in the receipt of a hundred dollars per month.

From the same cause an important branch of farming in Kansas and Missouri is the raising of stock. The Western expeditions absorb annually a very large number of oxen and mules. They, at the same time, furnish a valuable market for the consumption of the produce raised on the farms.

CHAPTER XVI.

THE white man's occupancy of Kansas is an event only of yesterday. So recently as August, 1854, it could be written that there was "not a town or village of whites in either Kansas or Nebraska." Till then these vast territories were, as they still in great part continue to be, the red man's hunting-grounds.

These Indian aborigines exist in great variety of tribes, and in almost equal variety of complexion, physical form, and degree of civilization, throughout the hundreds of thousands of square miles that lie between the United States and the Rocky Mountains. Very much, according to which of these tribes a traveller may fall in with, will be his impression as to whether the American Indians are living in a state of brutal debasement, and wasting away under the influence of vice and disease combined with frequent war and famine, or whether they are advancing in the arts of peace and civilization, and forming populous and happy commonwealths. I have myself witnessed, in tribes removed but a short distance from one another, the extremes of a brutality akin to that of the beast, and a civilization which might with advantage be copied by the white men in their neighbourhood. This remarkable difference of condition is not easily associated with the distinction of tribe, but is very readily connected with the diversity of circumstance and influence by which the particular tribe may have been surrounded.

Where no civilizing influence is brought to bear, the red man lives out his rude, savage life, hunting the buffalo and the elk, gorging himself when his chase is successful until he is insensible through repletion, and then awaking to spend days, perhaps, without a morsel of food; never cultivating the soil, but loving only the life of the nomade; ever warring against his neighbours of another tribe, and himself the victim of the most cruel superstitions and torturing fears. In such a state, there is no progress towards civilization. One generation goes and another comes, no whit the better than its predecessor, and often very much the smaller through famine or the ravages of smallpox, or through extermination by a more powerful tribe. Thus the Pawnees, who once spread over Kansas and Nebraska, to the number of nearly thirty thousand, and made other tribes submit to their power, have been reduced to a few thousand in number by visitations of smallpox, and by the superior power of the yet more savage Sioux, who have come down upon them from the North. Those that remain owe probably their existence to the fact that, in their weakness, they have accepted the protection of the whites, and have made some beginnings towards the possession of a civilized life.

Again, where—as is frequently the case—the relations of the white man to the Indian have

been accompanied by unhappy influences, the
result is seen in the red man knowing some-
thing of civilization, but knowing and imitating
only its vicious side.   Where there has been
tyranny and wrong on the part of the white
man, the Indian's native suspicion and vindictiveness have been confirmed and increased.
Where the Government agent has, with the one
hand, dealt out in large amount the annuities
voted by Congress, and with the other received
the money back in exchange for rum ; or where,
the agent being more honest, some speculating
trader has done his left hand's work for him ;
the result has been a fearful drunkenness, and the
growth of a passion which the Indian knows
not how to curb.   For a draught of the " fire-
water," the Indian will sometimes give all that
he has.   And it is undeniable that the cupidity
of the white man has dealt out destruction
amongst tens of thousands of the Indian race.

There are other ways besides, which it were
a shame to dwell upon, in which contact with
the races called civilized has only more bru-
talized the brutal, spread disease and death
among the red men's ranks, and given an out-

ward garniture of seeming civilization only to hide new shapes of vice and hideous deformity. Instances I need not give, for, to a greater or less degree, every Indian tribe is an example of the prejudicial influences of contact with the superior race. I may remark, however, as a further special illustration, that the half-breeds, wherever they exist in America, almost univerally exhibit a union of the vices of the two races whence they are derived, whilst their corresponding virtues are lost.

As I have looked at the white men with whom the aboriginal tribes have to deal, I have often wondered how any very happy influence upon the Indian character could be anticipated from their companionship and example.

But in some of the red races, civilization and Christian teaching have shown marvellous power. The instances just adverted to, where drunkenness and debauchery are the two chief lessons learned from association with the whites, are not instances of the failure of civilization and Christianity to elevate the savage, but of that which is not truly the one as it is eminently not the other. It would be very unfair, however, to charge the United States' Government with wholesale injustice, or even with neglect, in relation to the native tribes. Equally unfair would it be to bring its agents under a universal censure, as forgetful of the claims of humanity, and grasping only at self-advantage. It is true the history of the Indians in America, as from territory to territory they have been pushed out Westward before the advancing tide of white population, has been a most mournful one—mournful, I mean, not because they have had to yield to another race, but because of the barbarous cruelty with which the conquest has been, in former years at least, pursued. It were easy to gather from among the inhabitants of the States whole volumes of traditionary history as to the dealings of their fathers with the Indians; and nine-tenths of these traditions are traditions of bood, telling of the white man's cruelty and the red man's revenge. But for long the United States' Government has attempted to act honourably with the aboriginal possessors of the land. Congress votes yearly large sums as annuities to the dispossessed tribes. It sends an agent to arrange with the heads of the tribe for the sale of their land; and, although the Indians are not aware how disproportioned the sum offered is to the value of the land, still they accept the terms; and, fair or unfair as to the means by which the negotiation is concluded, the Government thus pays for what it takes. Further, it grants the dispossessed tribes reservations for their exclusive right. It establishes schools, sustains missions, provides farming implements and stock, introduces agriculture, and seeks to encourage labour and thrift, and thus to mould them into the habits of civilization.

Amongst the best examples of the happy effects of this mode of treatment, are those tribes which are now located in what is called the Indian Territory, immediately South of Kansas. This Territory contains a population of about a hundred thousand, principally Cherokees, Creeks, and Choctaws. These people have come under the influence of Christian teaching, and exhibit in a remarkable manner the fruits of the better policy adopted towards them. They have ceased to exist as tribes, and, possessing houses and farms, have formed themselves into a social order. Each nation has its own government, republican in form, and framed generally after the model of the United States. Each has its written constitution and laws. They have their public schools, education being provided for through their public funds. Large quantities of cotton and other produce are yearly sent by them to the New Orleans market. In the mechanical arts they have made considerable progress. The Scriptures and other books are in circulation in their own languages. The Cherokees and Choctaws each have their newspaper; and the former of these, being the most advanced, have two seminaries for higher instruction, as well as an orphan school—the former costing 70,000, the latter 18,000 dollars. Amongst the Cherokees are also some who have sought higher education in the universities of the States, and distinguished themselves by their attainments. And there are many who, as large planters, own negro slaves, for which practice they are also indebted to white civilization, and prove, I was informed, to be kind rather than tyrannical masters. These Indians are very anxious

to be in no particular behind their white neighbours, and look forward to their government
being recognized by the Confederacy, and
themselves admitted to representation in Congress.

According, therefore, as they have been
brought under elevating influences or otherwise, the Indians of North America may be
found, either living in the lowest depth of savage barbarism, steeped in the most loathsome
vice and misery, and dwindling away as a consequence of their corruption; or, on the other
hand, thriving and prosperous, possessing in
some degree the refined enjoyments, and ex-
hibiting the good fruits which belong to a
civilized condition.

Amongst the Indians inhabiting Kansas, may
be seen examples of almost every stage, from
the lowest to the highest. It is convenient to
classify the Indian tribes as indigenous and im-
migrant. The former are natives of the soil
they inhabit, and are commonly found in their
native debasement unaffected by civilizing influences. The latter belong originally to other
parts of the continent, now occupied by a large

and busy population, and have been transported
to the country they inhabit, or driven to it by
the Westward advance of the dominant race. It
is among these that the examples of a high
social condition to which I have adverted, are
to be found.

Of the tribes indigenous to Kansas, the most
numerous are the Kansas or Kaw Indians, from
which the Territory derives its name, who—
with the Osages in the Southern, and the Ot-
toes in the Northern portion of the Territory,
and some smaller tribes—make up the wild,
roving population which scours its Central and
Western plains. The Osages, all savage as
they are, honourably distinguish themselves by
their firm adherence to temperance principles.
Their abhorrence of the " fire-water" is very
remarkable, and is as rare as it is praiseworthy.
These tribes all speak dialects of the Dacotah
language, and thus identify themselves as members of the great family of the Sioux, one of the
most savage of the Indian tribes, which has
descended at different periods like a Northern
scourge, spreading its blood-thirsty armies for a
thousand miles over the savannahs of the West.

The Pawnees are a distinct race, and belong to Kansas, but are now much reduced in number. These, with the several Sioux tribes mentioned, form the native Indian population of Kansas, estimated at about eleven thousand, tenanting the broad open prairie, and often causing terror to the travellers crossing in the trains.

The Indian populations introduced from the East, and owning lands which have been assigned to them by the Government, are more numerous. They reach probably fourteen thousand. They vary much as to their degree of civilization. The fertile banks of the lower Kansas are cultivated by the Shawnees on the right or Southern bank, and by the Delawares and Wyandots on the North, following the margin of the Missouri as far as Leavenworth. The Shawnees have been well cared for, are good agriculturists, and have acquired generally the arts of civilized life. For fifty years the Society of Friends has sustained a Mission amongst them; and the Methodists and Baptists have likewise their schools for manual labor and instruction. The Wyandots are equally advanced. They own some beautiful lands, purchased from the Delawares, at the junction of the Kansas and Missouri rivers. They are remarkably fair in complexion, and I have met with many whose appearance, were they transported to our own country, would hardly betray their Indian origin. I journeyed for a week in company with a family of Wyandots, coming from one of the missions. The family consisted of two women, with several children, the eldest a grown lad. On board the steamboat, American etiquette, which is wonderfully tenacious of the rights of color, required that the Wyandot family should wait at each meal until every white passenger had eaten, when they were at liberty to sit down with the slaves and partake of whatever might remain. Yet they paid their full fare, and their deportment was a contrast in refinement to that of the self-styled " ladies," with whom they were accounted unworthy to sit at the same table.

Following the Missouri Northward from the Delaware reserve, we meet: first, the Kickapoos, a few miles from Fort Leavenworth; and upon their lands some few hundreds of Winnebagoes and Pottawatomies; further North, some of the Sacs and Foxes of Missouri; and, lastly, the Iowas, whose reservation reaches to the Nebraska border. The condition of the Iowas is very deplorable. They are of that class of Indians to whom contact with the whites, and participation in Government allowances, have wrought harm rather than good. They lead a life of miserable idleness, wear no dress beyond the blanket, and seem to set no value on efforts made for the amelioration of their condition.

Again, if we go from the Kansas river Southward, after passing the Shawnee reserve, we meet with the Pottawatomies, and small numbers of Weas and Piankeshaws, Peorias and Kaskaskias. These, with the Miamis, cluster about the banks of the Osage river and its tributaries. Further Westward, upon the Marais des Cygnes Creek, are to be found upwards of two thousand of the Sacs and Foxes from the Upper Mississippi. But more interesting is the small community of Ottowas and Chippewas, in the same district, whose condition a devoted Baptist missionary, the Rev. J. Meeker, has raised to one of a most encour-

aging character. The people have been induced
to give up their tribe system, and under the
stimulus of independent property, they advance
in numbers, in wealth, and, above all, in moral
and intellectual elevation. Further South, we
come upon the highly civilized Cherokees of
the Indian territory. The whole of these
reservations are in the Eastern portion of Kansas. And one effect of the rapid immigration of
white settlers which has taken place during
the last two years, will be, to dispossess many
of these Indians, to cause their transference
once more to a district further West.

Upon the whole, there is more to sadden
than to cheer in the aspect presented by the
Indian race on the Western plains of America.
In their natural condition, unutterably debased,
sunk almost to the level of the brute, their
contact with the white race has generally con-
tributed but little to their moral and social
elevation. Where the circumstances of this
contact, however rarely, have been more favourable, a different result is manifested, and in
instances of complete civilization, elements of
character are developed which command admi-

ration. There is sufficient in this to prove that the Red Indian is perfectly susceptible of elevating influences, and capable of being raised to his true position and dignity as a man; sufficient, therefore, to indicate the responsibility of the white man in relation to the race, and to call for a regret that the intercourse which has hitherto existed, has been of a character so little calculated to discharge that responsibility aright.

CHAPTER XVII.

Visit to a Company of Sioux Indians.—Their Crimes and
Punishment.—A timid Companion.—Ho! ho! ho! ho!—
Friendship accepted.—Friendship mistrusted.—Exhibition
of Displeasure.—The Calumet of Peace.—Indian Hospital-
ity.—Te-o-kún-ko's Appearance, Dress, and Feats.—Torn
Belly in a Blanket.—The Squaw and Pappoose.—Furnish-
ishings of the Tent.—Teaching the young Idea how to Shoot.
—Solemn Melancholy.—Parting Friendship.—Mother and
Child.—Description of Kansas Life concluded.—The Reign
of Terror.

ONE hot afternoon, having paid a visit at Fort
Leavenworth, I spent a while before returning
to the exciting scenes in the city, in strolling
about the grassy slopes and shady groves in
the neighbourhood of the Government reserve.
Suddenly my eye fell upon a little cluster
of tents, within a spacious inclosure, upon the
flank of a gently-swelling prairie-wave. As I
looked, there sprang from under one of the
tents a savage-looking figure, to whom paint
supplied the place of more seemly apparel.
The streaked and spotted savage darted forth

as if under some resistless impulse, raised his
arrow towards the sky, shot high and far, ran
for the fallen shaft, and returned to his hiding-
place, in less time than is needed to recount the
feat. Next appeared a woman, who crossed,
in her blanket, from one tent to another. I
knew at once that the Indians before me were
the company of Sioux of whom I had heard, an
hour previously, from Colonel Sumner.

These Sioux — belonging to the most savage
of the prairie tribes — had been guilty, during
the previous year, of stopping the mail on its
way across the plains to Utah, and of murdering
one of the officers in charge. It was not the
first occasion on which they had attacked parties
of travellers on the Western route. For this
act a number of the tribe implicated had been
taken as prisoners. Each man was privileged
to select from his wives the squaw of his choice ;
and the captive band had been conveyed to Fort
Leavenworth, and kept in confinement upon the
Government reserve. In the spring of 1856
the President granted them a pardon. Colonel
Sumner had the pleasing duty of ordering their
shackles to be knocked off, and of beholding

their gratitude in high leaps and joyous antics. They were now waiting an opportunity of convoy, by which they might be safely returned to their native wilds—the presence of many hostile tribes in the intervening territory being sufficient to make Fort Leavenworth a prison-house to them, from which they could not escape without a protecting force. Such was the history of this Dacotah band, as related to me by Colonel Sumner.

I crossed the fence and walked towards the tents, designing to form a more intimate acquaintance with the warrior tribe of which I had so often heard. I found I was not alone. A white man was looking from a distance at the lodges and their wild tenantry, whom I approached with the inquiry whether he had come to see the Indians. My white brother was not very communicative, but, on being pressed, said he was " took aback some, just a spot; he'd never sot eyes on such a salvagerous set of coons; he was nary lick afeared, not by a long sight, but he kinder druther keep tracks a little ways off such a salvagerous, onairthly set; they smelt so powerful bad." I told him

I comprehended his meaning, and placing myself between him and his supposed danger, induced him to accompany me round the side of the little encampment to get a front view of the tents and their occupants. In the mean time I told my companion briefly what I knew of the Indians; that they were Sioux, had attacked a train and committed murder, &c. My friend listened in silence.

We had examined from a short distance one or two interiors without attracting notice. At length we stood in front of a tent at some twenty yards distance, within which were two men, a woman, and a child. "Ho! Ho! Ho! Ho!" A shout, shrill and startling, showed that we were seen. It came from the head of the family; I cannot recall his name, but Te-o-kún-ko, the Swift, will answer the present purpose not inappropriately. The tall grim savage, who beyond a girdle had no covering except a thick sheathing of vermilion, ochre, and other pigments mingled with grease, sprang forward as he shouted, bow and arrow in hand, and made a beckoning motion with his arm. My companion was behind me, so that I was not in a position to see how the invitation affected him; but for myself, acting upon former experience, I accepted it immediately, and as I stepped quickly forward, found hands extended from within the tent, which I shook with a hearty cheerfulness.

But it was with Táh-zee-keh-dá-cha, the Torn Belly, and Tchón-su-móns-ka, the Sand-Bar, mistress of the lodge, in her robe of blue and belt of shining buttons, that I was shaking hands, for Te-o-kún-ko was already levelling his arrow at some offending object; on which he fixed an eye glaring with rage. I looked round, and to my horror discovered it to be none other than my companion, whom the shrill cry of the Sioux, half a minute before, had evidently pierced with terror, and who, panic-stricken, was "making tracks" as fast as his legs would bear him. Indians, thought I, never miss their aim. Te-o-kún-ko's rage was horrible to behold. A tragedy was surely to take place instantly before my eyes. No, a comedy! Te-o-kún-ko raises steadily his arrow towards the sky, whilst he bends his body backwards for a far upward shot. His head falls carelessly over his

shoulder towards his pale-faced guest, his countenance relaxes, the eye loses its fiery rage, and
with an unearthly "Ha! ha! ha!" the arrow
is sprung from the bow; it makes an acute
arc far up in the blue sky, and descends, as its
owner intended it should, at the feet of a horse,
midway between himself and the mean-spirited
runaway who had mistrusted his friendship.

I was now received into the family, and
honoured as a guest. There was little space to
spare beneath the tent; but he of the Torn
Belly, Táh-zee-keh-dá-cha, made me sit upon
the ground, and drew me close to his side, that
I might be sheltered from the scorching sun.
Te-o-kún-ko the meanwhile lit the calumet
of peace, and paid his guest the highest respect it is in the power of Indian host to
offer. The ugly, squat-shaped, broad-faced
child played about my feet; so I patted his wild
little head, and won the mother, Tchón-su-
móns-ka.

Te-o-kún-ko was of a restless disposition.
He never laid down his bow, but sprang out
frequently from beneath the tent to shoot an
arrow high aloft, run after it, and return. His

dress I have described in saying he had a blue girdle sustained by a leathern strap. He was tall, and of that extreme slenderness of limb only to be seen amongst certain wild races. His hair was parted in the centre, and brought down over each shoulder in a plait of two feet in length, into which horse-hair and other substances were introduced, and which terminated in a ball of thyme or other scented herb. Behind the head the hair was brought back, and terminated by a brass ring. He wore ear-rings; also a necklace of beads, long and short, alternately, and a second, looser necklace of brass chain. Further, he had armlets—five or six coils of stout brass wire above the elbow, two coils at the wrist. Each little finger had its ring. In his hand was his bow and a few arrows—the arrows broad at the point, and fledged with goose quill and other feathers brightly dyed. Other adornment had he none, save streaks of bright paint across his brow and cheeks, and spots and patches, red and yellow, about his naked body.

Táh-zee-keh-dá-cha, at my elbow, was a quiet sprite. He had a blanket loosely thrown around his shoulders; and whether he had lost his scalp or not, I cannot say, but he shielded his head with a handkerchief, which he held tightly beneath his chin. This attitude gave him very much the appearance of an old woman. He wore, also, beaded moccasins, and exhibited a larger number of finger-rings than his companion.

The squaw was dressed in a blue robe, which was held around her person by a broad leathern strap of unusual stoutness.. Had the intentions of its manufacturer been carried out, this strap would doubtless have found its place in the harnessing of some Western team; but it was now ornamented with a triple row of brass buttons, and put to fairer use. Sand-Bar had ear-rings, armlets, big and little finger-rings; her hair was parted and plaited, not wholly unlike that of any European; her forehead was daintily streaked with lines of beauty and grace, in bright blue and flaming vermilion.

The little pappoose was dressed simply in vest and leggins. From each ear hung two rings with watch-keys attached, the rings being

passed through both the lobe and the upper
cartilage of the ear.   Around its neck a brass
medal was suspended. On examining the medal,
I beheld the image and superscription of Queen
Victoria !

Behind the family group there hung, on the
sides of the tent, arrows, bows, pipes, furs,
buffalo-skins, painted robes, goose-quills, eagles'
claws and beaks, porcupines' spines, feathers,
hair, beads, paints, and all else that an Indian
counts valuable.   The complexion of these
Indians was of the darkest red, differing very
much in depth of shade from the more civilized
tribes.

As we could not exchange intelligibly a
single word, our intercourse was limited to
looks and gestures.   They examined my dress
with solemn curiosity.   The child began this,
and my neighbour, the Torn Belly, followed it
up.   He pulled my coat-tails, drew out my
neck-tie, pushed his finger up the same until
he tickled my neck, altogether surveyed me
thoroughly.   Afterwards we fell to amuse-
ment.   I stuck a coin upon a stick, and invited
the pappoose to shoot with his miniature bow

and arrow. The young Sioux warrior entered into the game with zest, his father sustaining his arm, whilst he again and again shot only to miss the mark. At last he won his prize, gave the bit of silver into his mother's keeping—an office which she discharged by putting it into her mouth—and eagerly demanded a renewal of the practice.

Through the half-hour during which I sat under their tent, these solemn figures never smiled, never indicated in the countenance the least presence of feeling. Even the child never laughed. When it triumphed with the bow, the father said, "Ha! ha! ha!" and the child said, "He! he! he!" but the countenances never relaxed their mournful expression. Every Indian that I ever saw, has exhibited the same strange characteristic. The red races are said to be cheerful, even jovial, amongst themselves. Be this true or false, in the presence of strangers they divest themselves of every indication of the emotional, and leave upon the mind an impression of the profoundest melancholy.

When I rose to go, my entertainers shook me

warmly by the hand, and indicated their desire that I should repeat my visit, and especially remember to bring some tobacco with me the next time. Having passed behind the tent, I heard a foot-step following me. It was the little marksman, who, when I stopped, ran towards me, and seized my legs as if to detain me. Next came the Sand-Bar, rushing to the rescue, lest white man should steal red man's child. I surrendered that which it would have been a sore affliction to keep, and left, convinced, that whether under a white skin or a red one, a mother's heart is still the same.

When I returned from my friendly visit to the Sioux to the riot and savage turmoil of the white settlement, I felt doubtful whether I had not left civilization behind me.

With these Indian sketches, however, my description of the country and its inhabitants must terminate. Much indeed remains unsaid, which is characteristic of Kansas and its home-life in town and country. But having yet to treat more particularly of the fierce struggle between slavery and freedom of which it has been the theatre, and to supply some passages in its brief but stormy history, I must close this portion of the subject. It is impossible, however, to leave the consideration of its beautiful prairies and fertilizing streams, its busy settlers and active commerce, without giving expression to the mournful regret, that a country on which Nature smiles so beautifully, and towards which Providence has been so bountiful in the gifts of material wealth and natural advantages, should have been turned by the foul hand of man into a land of sorrow and suffering, bloodshed and crime. Now the widow wrings her hands, and orphans shed tears of bitterness over that rich and lovely soil; discord and anarchy have taken the place of law; poverty and partial famine are seen instead of abundance; wrong has been legalized, right subdued; and, amid the heavings of an uncontrolled lawlessness, men have cast from them every moral restraint, and introduced a Reign of Terror, in which every base passion of man finds free exercise for its energies of evil.

CHAPTER XVIII.

The Controversy.—Shall Kansas be Slave or Free?—Slavery
a Barrier to a Country's Advancement.—Influence of Slavery on Population, Education, Cultivation of the Soil, Price
of Land.—A fair Competition would make Kansas Free.—
Pecuniary and Political Interests of the South.—A fair Competition from the first denied.

IT is strange that men should fight so hard to
introduce so bad a thing as slavery into a land.

We have been so accustomed to dwell on
the moral evils of slavery, the essential enormity of the system, and the wrongs which
almost of necessity arise out of it, that we are
apt to overlook that which otherwise we
should not be slow to recognize, namely, how
baneful the system is in its influence upon the
white race, and how seriously it impoverishes
a country, and retards the progress of its people.

The celebrated Jefferson, himself a slaveholder, has left in his writings a strong testimony against the system in its reflex influence

upon the masters, when he said, that "the man must be a prodigy who can retain his manners and morals undepraved" whilst living in the midst of such a system. "The whole commerce," he writes, "between master and slave is a perpetual exercise of the most boisterous passions—the most unremitting despotism on the one part, and degrading submission on the other." As one of the chief founders of the republic, Jefferson,—in common with Washington, Franklin, Madison, Henry, and all the leaders of his time,—regarded the abolition of what he calls "this great political and moral evil," as essential to the prosperity of the Union.

But slavery is as great an economical, as it is a political or moral evil. The day on which I first set foot in a slave state, and a few hours before I crossed the border-line, I was conversing with a gentleman residing in Pennsylvania, whose views appeared to be Southern, but who expressed them in a tone of candour and moderation. "Well," said he at length, "this afternoon you will be in our Southern states. You expect, I dare say, to find the difference the moment you cross the state-line. Whichever way you look, you will calculate on seeing nothing but what is bad. I should like very much to know, whether you find it as bad as it is most likely you expect."

The truth is, I had no expectation to "feel the difference the moment I crossed the state-line." I was not prepared for any visible sign of the geographical boundary being passed. How great, then, was my surprise to find that, in going into a state naturally richer, I was in effect entering one practically and visibly poorer; and that the enterprise and progress I had been accustomed to admire in the Northern states, were exchanged, on the passing of a geographical line, for lethargy and almost back-going. It was evident that I was in the midst of new conditions of society, and that new social conditions had brought with them a wholly new and widely different order of things, one that reached the length of changing the entire aspect of the country. Had I met my friend afterwards, I must have confessed to many and great surprises; and, had he asked me my opinion as to the "institution" after travelling throughout the Southern states,—passing the moral evil—I must have characterized it, as a visible blight upon the entire economical and commercial, as well as social, existence of the South.

Now in Kansas we have a country, immense in extent and most rich in its capabilities of production, till recently guaranteed to be free from this blighting influence as well as great wrong, but now thrown open to its unrestrained introduction. In the persons of their respective advocates, the rich soil of Kansas has become the battle-ground of the two systems, Slavery and Freedom. All who have interest in the progress of humanity, and many besides, ask anxiously, which is to be the victor ? Is slavery to find in it a new soil over which to extend its pernicious influence, or are the energies of freemen to make it a land which shall smile with the blessings of social happiness and general prosperity ?

By all unprejudiced witnesses the fact is acknowledged, that slave labour in any temperate climate cannot hold its ground when brought into fair competition with free labour.

As a system, slavery ever brings with it a heavy entail of disorder, slovenly negligence, stereotyped adhesion to old methods, disregard of all improvements, costly and unnoticed expenditure, and general impoverishment in all that pertains to the cultivation of the soil.

This is not a matter of controversy. It is sufficient to see the " thrown out" or " turned out" lands of Virginia,—thousands of acres now no longer cultivated, naturally far richer than the soil of Massachusetts, enjoying a more genial climate, adapted to the growth of more remunerative products, and in a state colonized at an earlier period,—and to compare the poverty of the one with the wealth exhibited in the other state, to be convinced of the terribly pernicious influence of the slave system on the agriculture of a country. Whether we illustrate the contrast between a slave state and a free state, in the market price of the land, in the difference of population, or in the relative extent of unimproved soil, we arrive at the same conclusion, and gain sure indices of the prejudicial economic results of slavery.

To cross the border from Pennsylvania to

Virginia, is to cross from land at forty-nine
dollars, to land at twenty-one dollars per acre,
as shown by the Government returns. In
South Carolina, with its far-famed rice plantations, the returned value of the land is only a
fraction over five dollars per acre; in free Connecticut, it is upwards of thirty dollars the
acre. Or, passing to the states of the West, it
would be sufficient for intending settlers in
Kansas to glance at the neighbouring slave
state of Missouri. They would there see the
twelve southern counties in that state showing
in the Government returns a value for their
land of thirteen dollars per acre; whilst its
ten northern counties, bordering on free Iowa,
although naturally less productive, support a
population one-fourth larger; that population
has improved one-half more of soil; has raised
the soil it has improved to a value about
one-half higher, namely, nineteen dollars an
acre; and is possessed, as a consequence, of an
assessed value in land two and a half times as
large as that of the finer counties in the south
of the same state. It may further be mentioned that, for 339 scholars in the public schools

in the twelve southern counties, the ten counties bordering on Iowa can show a school attendance of 2,329. Yet this is but the result of the proximity of freedom

And if the slave system, as contrasted with free labour, is always accompanied by an inferior agriculture, a depreciated value of the land, a smaller population, a fettered commerce, and a remarkable prevalence of almost barbarous ignorance, there are yet further many special reasons why slavery should not be permitted to introduce its paralyzing influence upon the free soil of Kansas. The climate is temperate; hence those products for the raising of which negro slavery is sometimes claimed to be necessary, are not grown on its soil. Slave labour, again, is unprofitable, except where the slaves can work in gangs, and can be kept within the view of the overseer. Hence, the Indian corn and other grain crops which are best adapted to the soil and climate of Kansas, are quite unsuitable for any but free labour. Further, of planters owning slaves, but a small number can be expected for many years to come to transport their stock into this new territory, whilst the remaining settlers, even from the South, are not necessarily slave-pro-prietors.

From a consideration of facts such as these, the conclusion has been drawn, that Kansas left to itself (as is guaranteed by the Organic Act, passed in May, 1854) to determine its own institutions, and to legalize or not to legalize slavery, according to the will of the majority, must inevitably determine in favour of freedom. Some writers, even in this country, have with too much haste concluded, that so unequal a race as that between slavery and freedom cannot be long sustained; that, with the pernicious fruits of slave labour before their eyes, the settlers in Kansas cannot long hesitate in their choice; that the territory must soon, therefore, settle down, and make its application for admission into the confederacy with a constitution guaranteeing freedom. Hence these writers infer, moreover, that, if the strife existing in Kansas has disturbed the whole Union, the anxiety exhibited on both sides is very unnecessary,—at any rate on the part of the North,—seeing that very speedily, by the working out of natural causes, Kansas must of necessity become free.

Such a conclusion, reasonable as it may appear, is founded on an imperfect view of the question. The question is not whether Kansas ought to be a free or a slave state, in order best to secure its ultimate prosperity and the development of its resources; but whether Kansas, free or slave, will most enrich those who are able to profit by its being opened to them. In a case like that of Kansas, the most profitable will be always deemed, by the majority of men, the most reasonable policy. And as the majority are to rule, the question reduces itself to this : Is there not a large class to whom the extension of slavery is a source of profit? And if so, is that class in preponderating number?

Whilst it is perfectly true, therefore, that between slavery and freedom in Kansas, it is a folly on material, as much as it is a wrong on moral grounds, to choose the former, it is not to be forgotten that the self-interest of many may conflict with the requirements of right reason. In concluding that men can never

commit the folly of making Kansas a slave
state, we lose sight of the important fact, that
the South has an immense interest in upholding
slavery and in extending it over new territory.
The history of slavery in the United States
has always been ultimate loss for the sake of
present gain; an impoverished inheritance left
to the child for the sake of immediate profit
to the father. To supply the depreciation consequent on the land being left almost to itself,
and, therefore, not rising in value, it is of
immense importance to the planters of the
South, that the value of their slave-property
should be maintained, and, if possible, increased.
Though a fictitious source of wealth, a rise in
the price of his slaves is of more importance
to the planter than a rise in the value of his
land, in proportion as he has more money invested in the one than in the other. To
bring about this result there is no means so
effectual as the extension of slave territory,
which is, in effect, the opening of a new market for the slaves.

Virginia alone is drawn upon by the states
on the Mississippi, for as many as ten thousand

annually,— a rare encouragement, it must be confessed, for slave-breeding.

Governor Wise is reported to have told the Virginians that, if California were made a slave state, the value of their negroes would rise from a thousand to three, or even five, thousand dollars.

Every slaveholder, therefore, has a direct immediate interest in the extension of the area of slavery, although it should bring eventual ruin to the development of the country's resources. Add to this, that to gain fresh political power is of highest moment to the Southern interest. The ascendancy of the North is an event the slaveholder with reason dreads, as likely, if not to jeopardize his property, at least to curtail his privileges. Hence the favour with which he regards all filibustering, Southern annexation, and extension of slave territory in general. Every new slave state admitted to the confederacy gives two more votes for slavery in the Senate, and a further addition to Southern votes in the House of Representatives, besides engaging another whole population in the support of the Pro-slavery interest. More need

not be said, to show that, if the voice of the
South were to decide it, Kansas would be
given not to freedom, but to slavery.

But the truth is, the question extends itself
far beyond the limits of Kansas. The ultimate
fate of this territory will very materially influence the subsequent history of territories beyond, as well as of states in its neighbourhood.
With all its vehemence in the cause, Missouri
is not strong as a slave state; its northern portion is eminently unfitted for slave labour;
and, if Kansas were to be made a free state,
Missouri itself, having free soil on its north,
west, and east, would probably ere long become to a great extent practically free. Again,
with a free Kansas, freedom must be given of
necessity to Nebraska, and whatever other new
states may be formed north of the old compromise line. Hence, Kansas is made the
battle-ground of a great principle. " Squatter
sovereignty," forced upon the country by the
abettors of Southern views, must there work
itself out to its legitimate issues; and the
issue with relation to Kansas will, to a great
extent, determine the ultimate condition of the

other vast territorial possessions of the American Union.

It is of yet greater significance, however, to remark, that the supposition that in Kansas the slave system must yield eventually to free labour, is unfounded, because, from its first settlement, two years ago, this fair competition between the two systems of labour has never been permitted. An equal race would, unquestionably, result in the triumph of freedom; but this has been from the first denied. The partisans of the South, insisting on their own views, have proscribed all opposition; and possessing the aid and authority of the federal Government, have decreed that nothing shall be legal which does not favour their own side in this contest of principles.

To reveal the base infamy of these transactions,—transactions in which the Government at Washington is as deeply implicated as the border-ruffians of Missouri—as well as to exhibit the revolting barbarity which has been associated with them, I invite attention to the brief history of the Kansas struggle contained in the following chapters. A consideration of its varied events will suffice, I think, to carry the conviction that a fair competition between the systems of slavery and freedom has not hitherto existed, and by those in power was never intended to exist, in Kansas.

CHAPTER XIX.

The Commencement of the Troubles in Kansas.—Its Organization as a Territory.—Slavery prohibited previously by the Missouri Compromise.—Senator Douglas.—Conception of a bold Idea.—The Compact broken.—Passing of the Nebraska-Kansas Act.—Squatter Sovereignty.—Unskilled Legislators.—The people to regulate their Domestic Institutions in their own Way.—Mr. Seward's Speech.

KANSAS dates the commencement of its troubles from the day on which the Act was passed by the Congress of the United States, which gave it a political existence as a duly organized Territory. This was in May, 1854.

Its previous history in relation to slavery was very simple. In virtue of what is commonly called the Missouri Compromise Measure of 1820, the North conceded to the South that Missouri, which lies north of latitude 36° 30′, should be admitted into the Union as a slave state; accepting as an equivalent the enactment, that in all the remaining portion of the Louisiana Territory lying north of that geographical line, slavery "shall be and is hereby for ever prohibited." Kansas is north of that line of latitude, which very accurately divides the northern from the southern half of the possessions of the United States. The question was finally, and for ever, settled by a strictly defined line, confirmed by many subsequent acts of legislation. And thus, for four and thirty years, Kansas had peace.

Prominent among those of Northern politicians in America, who are devoted to Southern interests, is the Honourable Stephen Arnold Douglas. Mr. Douglas is a short, thick-set man, of dark complexion, determined in action, and vehement in speech; but withal clever, full of tact and ability, and well fitted to carry whatever measure he may set his heart upon. He was, it is understood, in his earlier career a labouring man or mechanic; and, it is probable, set his heart upon the Presidential Chair. At any rate, he has made great steps towards the attainment of that coveted honour. Still a young man, he has risen from his lowly station, and now sits as Senator for Illinois. It

would be a pleasing reflection, if this rapid
elevation had taken place side by side with
independent action and faithfulness to the
great trust of one who rules his country.
Probably Mr. Douglas may say, he has been
faithful to his own convictions. Still, the
truth remains:—A Northern man, he has
espoused Southern politics; swimming with
the stream of official favour, he has, in be-
friending those in power, most befriended himself; he has struck well for the highest honour
America has to bestow, and, having achieved a
great past, has opened for himself the way,
should fortune still favour, for a great future;
finally, he may take to himself the credit of
having made more noise than almost any other
member of the Senate in the present Congress,
and having done more by public acts to influence his country—albeit that influence is to
curse it—than probably any man of his time.

Senator Douglas, as a trusty servant of the
South and friend of the Administration, sat as
Chairman upon the Committee of Territories.
When, in December, 1853, a bill was sub-
mitted by Mr. Dodge, Senator for Iowa, for

the organization of the Territory of Nebraska, Mr. Douglas took the bill in hand in committee, and returned it to the House amended, in the shape of a wholly new bill. The little alteration he had to suggest was nothing less than that the Compromise of 1820 should be revoked, or rather that it should be held to be inoperative and void, because Congress had no right to legislate upon the subject of slavery,[*] and that the new territories should be placed under that peculiar rule now known as Squatter Sovereignty. What rewards are great enough for the daring ingenuity that devised, and the energy that carried through the House, a measure like this, contemplating ends which minds cast in the ordinary mould would never have ventured even to conceive!

Such genius was irresistible. The man being found who had the hardihood to say, " Let us break faith and we can carry all our own way," the scheme had not to wait for willing adherents. From thirty to seven-and-thirty voted at the different divisions in favour of the

[*] In the territories, that is to say.—AM. ED.

measure; from ten to fourteen were all who opposed it in the Senate. A majority was likewise found for it in the House of Representatives. And thus the bill, which broke a compact solemnly entered into, for which an equivalent had been received, and which had often been reaffirmed,—a bill which declared impossible that which was enacted " for ever," and had been acted upon for thirty-four years, became the law of the land.

By virtue of another provision of the substituted bill, the great tract of country formerly called somewhat indefinitely Nebraska, was divided into two distinct territories; the more promising portion at the south, bordering on the State of Missouri, being organized under the name of Kansas, and the remaining portion, reaching as far north as the British possessions, receiving the specific title of the Territory of Nebraska. This was sagacious, even as all the other provisions of the Act. To subjugate to the slave power a territory stretching so far north as the orignal Nebraska, would have been an almost hopeless task. To fight the battle on a comparatively narrow strip of country in the south, with Missouri on its entire flank from south to north, was a task comparatively easy and full of promise as to ultimate success.

Thus was Kansas organized as a Territory of the Union, under the dominion of that new form of government known, in modern history, as "Squatter Sovereignty." In the settlement of all new territory, there is in most instances a period during which, the surveys being yet uncompleted, men are found to throw down their hatchet upon land to which as yet they have no title. Such men are called squatters. Much almost inevitable evil springs out of this system, as has been shown in former parts of this volume. For purposes of mutual defence, societies are formed, understandings are come to, and thenceforward all is regulated in accordance with "Squatter Law," and for the maintenance of "Squatter Rights." There exists little definable distinction between Squatter law and Lynch law; and when men speak of holding land by Squatter right, they often mean what is otherwise expressed as Tomahawk right.

When General Cass first made use in the Senate of the expression "Squatter Sovereigns," he had reference to the legalization of power in the hands of the class of men above described. Uncertain as to their dwelling-place, unpossessed of titles to their so-called "claims," believing in law only so far as it favours themselves, as unskilled in relation to the principles of justice as they are unscrupulous in the methods of its administration, it might be reasonably supposed that the squatters are not the best men to constitute the rulers of the land. Yet, according to the enlightened legislation of the last few years, the squatters have been made the sovereigns through most of the territories of the United States.

Kansas is an example of the legitimate working out of the much admired system of squatter sovereignty. By the Act organizing it as a territory, it was stipulated that, whilst the compact under which it had been guaranteed free from slavery since 1820 was to be held as inoperative and void, the people were to be at liberty to "form and regulate their domestic institutions in their own way." The squatter

sovereigns, being very far from harmonious in
their views of the peculiar domestic institution
intended by this expression, have been quite
unable to agree as to how it is to be regulated,
and have very naturally resorted to fighting, in
order to decide whether slavery is to be legislated into, or excluded from, the territory.

Mr. Seward, the Senator for New York, was
not far from the truth, when, on the memora-
ble night of the passing of the Nebraska-Kansas Bill, he closed his fruitless opposition to it,
by designating the act of that night as one that
would mark an era in American legislation.
"We are on the eve of the consummation of a
great national transaction—a transaction which
will close a cycle in the history of our country—and it is impossible not to desire to pause
for a moment, and survey the scene around us
and the prospect before us. * * * The sun has
set for the last time upon the guaranteed and
certain liberties of all the unsettled and unor-
ganized portions of the American continent
that lie within the jurisdiction of the United
States. To-morrow's sun will rise in dim
eclipse over them." How long the obscuration

would last, Mr. Seward continued to say, no human mind could foresee. One thing is certain : the Senator's prophecy of a coming darkness has been verified in Kansas to the full; from the moment of the passing of that bill there has been nothing but darkness, thick darkness enwrapping the land ; and the light has scarcely yet even faintly begun to dawn.

CHAPTER XX.

Missouri takes an Interest in Kansas.—Claims staked off.—
Sovereignty taken up in the new Territory.—Blue Lodges.
—Slavery " at whatever Cost of Blood and Treasure."—Hostile Resolutions.—Indian Lands ceded.—Northern Immigration.—The Challenge accepted.—Appointment of Governor
and Judiciary.—Governor Reeder.—Lawrence founded.—
Leavenworth and other Settlements.—Election of Delegate
to Congress.—The Contest.—Missourian Invasion.—General
Stringfellow's Programme of Operations.—Return of General Whitfield.

AT the time when Kansas was thus organized
and opened for settlement, the inhabitants of
the contiguous State of Missouri had very much
their own way in the new Territory. For
some time previously, they seem to have been
possessed of the secret, that the Compromise of
1820 was to be broken, and that the squatter
was to have the sovereignty of Kansas. Accordingly, most of those living near the border
took occasion, at some time or other, to cross
the river, and " stake off a claim." This was

done in order to give them the sovereignty
they desired. Each man, although his "stak-
ing off a claim" should have consisted merely
in pacing out forty acres and leaving a notch
with his axe on one of the trees, considered
himself thereby constituted a squatter, and
invested consequently with a share in the sovereignty of the future Territory. Each man
also agreed to respect the rights of his brother-
squatter. This is part of squatter law; and is
self-evidently the only condition on which to
have one's own right maintained. "If you
will say I am lord of the soil, I will say you
are; and so, we shall be all lords together, and
none, who is not of our way, shall invade our
sovereign right." Whilst each recognized his
brother-squatter, it occurred apparently to no
one to respect the rights of the Indian tribes.
These not merely occupied the land, but had
had the land specially assigned to them by
the government in compensation for their removal from, and surrender of possessions,
further East. Hence, the "claims," on which
these inhabitants of Missouri rested their right
to rule Kansas, had the additional detraction

that the land which, although unpaid for, they called their own, belonged by public treaty to other people.

At about the period of the passing of the act, " blue lodges" and other secret societies were formed; and, throughout the year 1854, numerous meetings were held in Western Missouri, at which the people were addressed by General David R. Atchison, then Vice-president of the United States,* General Stringfellow, Dr. Bayless and others. Thus a powerful movement was organized, having for its object the settlement of Kansas by the people of Missouri, and the exclusion of all emigrants from the North.

At the earlier of these meetings, the people "pledged themselves, if the territory of Kansas be opened to settlement, to co-operate to extend the institutions of Missouri [i. e. slavery] over the territory, *at whatever cost of blood and treasure.*" And, as they were ready before the opening of the territory, to shed their blood

---

* He had been elected President of the Senate in place of W. R. King, V. P., in December, 1852.—AM. ED.

that slavery might be introduced, so at a later period, when settlers began to come from the North under the protection of Eastern Emigrant Aid Societies, they encouraged each other by resolutions still more violent, and meetings more directly hostile in their character. At the meetings of the " Platte County Self-defensive Association" and other similar organizations, the resolutions generally adopted were to the effect, that protection should be afforded to none but Southern settlers in Kansas; that Abolitionists arriving there should be immediately removed from the territory; and that all coming from any place North of Mason and Dixon's line were Abolitionists, and to be treated as such, whatever they might say to the contrary.

In the mean time arrangements were made by the government for the cession of lands by the Indians. This was not effected in the ordinary manner, by a commissioner appointed to negotiate with the tribes on their own soil. But delegates from the Indians were taken privately to Washington, a treaty negotiated with them, and information immediately telegraphed to the Missouri associations, which were ready at once to take up the ceded lands. Much complaint was made by the Indians afterwards in relation to these treaties. " The chiefs, head men, and counsellors of the Delaware nation" published also a protest against the acts of " their white brethren," in settling on lands in violation of the treaties made with them. But the Missourians had gained their end. They had, by their interest at Washington, obtained precedence of the Northern men in taking up the lands. They held large districts under squatter right ; and under the sovereignty of squatterdom, they considered themselves possessed of authority to rule, if need were, the Indians out, and to legalize themselves in.

There was activity, however, on the part of the free States. The State of Massachusetts especially showed itself energetic in promoting the settlement of Kansas by its own New England sons. In this, they accepted the challenge which the principle of the Nebraska-Kansas act offered, and showed themselves willing to run the race with the South, encouraged by the idea that the majority of the population of

the new Territory was to decide the question
of its institutions.   Hence sprung the Massachusetts Emigrant Aid Society, and the American Settlement Company of New York, as well
as minor associations, known as the Octagon
Settlement Company, the Vegetarian Settlement Company, and the New York Kansas
League.   The object of these associations was
to assist settlers in Kansas by making arrangements for their transit, aiding them in the
choice of locations, and especially enabling
them, by an advance of capital, to erect sawmills and other valuable appendages, for general use.   As a consequence of this agency, and
tempted by the increased advantages of protection and comfort which settlement held out
under the operation of such a system, large
numbers from the free States were induced to
make Kansas their home.   And the Territory
still presents, in consequence of the peculiarities of its history, a contrast of population very
unusual in the Far Western lands.   On the one
hand are those in great number who by their
thoughts and feelings, habitudes and wants,
indicate that they have been nursed amidst the

social refinements of New England or New York, and that Western life is yet strange to them; and on the other hand, in constant contact with these, there are exhibitions of savage coarseness and brutality, which are happily rare even amidst the rough forest-life of the first pioneers.

By the Organic Act, the Governor and Judiciary of the Territory were to be appointed by the President of the United States. Mr. Andrew H. Reeder of Pennsylvania received the appointment as head of the Executive, with Mr. Daniel Woodson of Arkansas, as Secretary. Samuel Dexter Lecompte was made Chief Justice of the Territory, with Sanders N. Johnston and Rush Elmore as Associate Justices, and Isaacs and Donaldson respectively Attorney and Marshal. These were all appointed as unflinching supporters of the Southern cause. Some of them have remarkably justified whatever was expected of them. But Reeder, the Governor, appears from the first to have hesitated to yield himself as the instrument of giving effect to the base designs of the Missourian party. He exhibited a caution and reserve, which were very becoming in one holding the highest civil power in the Territory, but which were very unpalatable to those who looked to him for plain-spoken, unshrinking partisanship. In his public acts, he seemed to aim at impartiality. In speech, he always avoided committing himself, and as to any expression of his opinions or intentions observed strict silence. He probably found the abettors of the principle of Squatter Sovereignty to be men very different in character from that which he had anticipated; and shrinking from allying himself with a border-ruffian horde, he soon became mistrusted by the party he was expected to support, and thus prepared the way for his dismissal from his office.

The Governor arrived in the territory early in October, 1854. During the two or three months preceding, settlers had been entering at a rapid rate; and at a pretty spot on the Southern bank of the Kansas river, some forty miles from its mouth, a number of Free-state emigrants had founded what is now called the City of Lawrence. In July, 1854, consisting of but a single log-hut; in October, comprising

a score, or thereabouts, of rough wooden tenements, within which its inhabitants had to
make their bed upon the floor with buffalo-robe
and blanket; Lawrence has since risen to the
dignity of a city, possesses the best buildings
in the territory, has its public edifices, supports
several newspapers, has its literary society, is
protected, moreover, by earthwork fortifications,
has twice sustained a siege, and has achieved for
itself a history and a name. At about the same
time, the foundations were laid of Topeka,
Pawnee, Grasshopper Falls, and other places,
which being the work of Free-state settlers,
called forth the jealousy and threatened hostility
of the opposing party. The Southern men who
"moved into" Kansas, settled chiefly in Leavenworth, and at Kickapoo, Atchison, Doniphan,
and other places upon the Missouri, conveniently
near to the State from which they principally
came. Leavenworth, although now a " City,"
had not yet probably more than a dozen houses;
but it became a great centre for land speculators, and, with its advantages as a point for
commerce, has experienced a wonderfully rapid
growth.

Each organized Territory of the United States is permitted to be represented in Congress by one delegate, who has liberty to speak, but possesses no voting power. One of the first duties of Governor Reeder, on arriving in Kansas, was to appoint a day for the election of the Territorial Delegate. He appointed Nov. 29, divided the territory into nineteen electoral districts, and appointed judges for each district, who were to administer the oaths, especially that of actual residence, and to preside generally over the election. The candidates for the office were three: Mr. Whitfield, the nominee of the border counties of Missouri, a tall, determined-looking man, whose antecedent history belonged to the annals of Indian trading; Judge Wakefield, a plain-spoken and thorough Free-soiler, a man who had been a long lifetime in the West, and possesses the respectable and comfortable appearance which belongs to the portly judge of olden time; and Mr. Flenniken, theoretically an advocate of squatter sovereignty, who had accompanied Governor Reeder into the territory, and held views probably not far differing from his own.

The election day came, and with it the first day of that open violence which has since plunged Kansas into so much misery. General Whitfield was the nominee of the people of Missouri. By fair means or by foul, he must be elected. The "Blue Lodge" gathered its forces, summoned to its aid its secret pass-words, signs, and grips, and speedily had obtained means, and mustered forces sufficient to control the election in the neighbouring territory. They could not but be successful; for, although all the legal votes that were recorded in the territory had been given undividedly to either of the other candidates, there were yet as many, and more than half as many more, friends of slavery who came to secure the victory to Whitfield. Independently, however, of this overwhelming number of illegal votes, General Whitfield had a majority. A very large proportion of the settlers did not vote: others were ignorant of Whitfield's true character, and voted for him. In Kansas he had declared himself to be in favour of the people deciding their institutions for themselves, according to the true theory of squatter sovereignty,—that is, A governing A.

This gained him votes. Afterwards it proved that he was in favour of the institutions of Kansas being decided by the people of Missouri, —that is, B governing A.

In this election the Missourians were lavish in their provision for a thorough conquest. One might suppose that in a district like Marysville, which at the best could scarcely boast of more than half a dozen log-houses, 238 armed men were not needed in order to carry the poll. Yet 238 went thither, and recorded their votes for Whitfield, against seven residents voting for the other candidates. In all, the 1729 who were subsequently recognized by the Committee of Investigation as non-resident voters, appear to have spread their force over eight of the electoral districts. It· is needless to say they conquered.

These invaders from Missouri made no concealment of their purpose in visiting Kansas; they freely said that they intended to make Kansas a slave state. Where the judges were not compliant, they removed them, and extemporized judges from their own number. Some, to make a show of residence, struck a stake into the ground, or nailed a piece of paper with their name upon it to a tree, or entered their names upon lists as persons who meant to settle in Kansas at some time. All, if their own statements be relied on, either had a " claim," or intended to have a " claim," or had some friend who had a " claim ;" and therefore all had votes. And a great portion not only had votes for themselves, but votes for friends also, left behind probably in Missouri, but who were going to settle in Kansas, and, wishing to have a hand in shaping the laws and institutions of the territory, had asked them to vote for them.

In the majority of instances, it was sufficient to surround the approach to the balloting-box with a crowd of armed ruffians to deter the Free-state men from voting. A few days previously their operations had been marked out for them by General Stringfellow. They were to " mark every scoundrel that was the least tainted with free-soilism or abolitionism, and to exterminate him ;" they were to have no " qualms of conscience as to violating laws, state or national, the time had come when such impositions must be disregarded ;" they were to " enter every election district in Kansas, in defiance of the Governor and his vile myrmidons, and vote at the point of the bowie-knife and the revolver ;" they were to " crush out the abolition rascals," and to " mind that slavery be established." " It was enough that the slaveholding interest willed it, from which there is no appeal.'

And that day, the 29th of November, 1854, the slaveholding interest, from which there is no appeal, achieved the first of its great bowie-knife victories, and witnessed the establishment of rifle-rule in Kansas.

CHAPTER XXI.

Election for the Territorial Legislature, March 30, 1855.—Spirit of the Press.—Preparations for an Invasion in Missouri.—Numbers of the Invading Forces.—The Hemp.—Incidents of Bowie-knife Voting.—Ninety out of every Hundred Votes Illegal.—Incidents at Bloomington.—Sheriff Jones' Exploits.—Windows Smashed.—House Lifted.—Ballot-box Stolen.—Hurrah for Missouri!—Returning Home.—Piratical Symbols.—Victory.—Protests against Elections.—Unpopularity of Governor Reeder.—Summary Punishment of a Newspaper Press.—The Fraudulent Legislature Organized.—Exclusion of Free-state Members.—Two Months of Legislation.— Appointment of Officers.—Reciprocity. — Public Companies.

THE next event of importance in the history of Kansas was the election of members of council and representatives to form a Territorial Legislature. This was fixed for March 30, 1855.

During the interval, nothing was done either to rectify past illegalities, or to pacify the ill-feeling which thence resulted. The temper of the men of influence in Missouri may be gathered from their public papers. The *Squatter Sover-cign*, Dr. Stringfellow's organ, published at Atchison, reflects the spirit of the Pro-slavery men as follows :—

"Monday of last week a fight came off at Doniphan, Kansas territory, in which bowie-knives were used freely. The difficulty arose out of a political discussion, the combatants being a Pro-slavery man and a Free-soiler. Both parties were badly cut, and we are happy to state that the Free-soiler is in a fair way to 'peg out,' while the Pro-slavery man is out and ready for another tilt. Kansas is a hard road for Free-soilers to travel."

Again, in their editorial columns :—

"We can tell the impertinent scoundrels of the *Tribune*, that they may exhaust an ocean of ink, their emigrant aid societies spend their millions and billions, their representatives in Congress spout their heretical theories till doomsday, and his Excellency Franklin Pierce appoint Abolitionist after Free-soiler as our governor, yet we will continue to lynch and hang, to tar and feather, and drown every white-livered Abolitionist who dares to pollute our soil."

When the 30th March came, the leaders of the Pro-slavery party were prepared for it by a thorough organization, extending through all the Western counties of Missouri, as a result of which they were enabled to pour into the Territory of Kansas an invading force, in comparison of which that called out on the former occasion was small.

The voters were marshalled into distinct bands under separate leadership. Those that were to exercise the suffrage in more remote districts, mounted their horses and got ready their waggons a few days in advance. Every warlike equipment was provided, and on the day of election, the testimony from Lawrence tells us, they were seen upon the field, marching to the sound of drum, with banners waving in the wind, plentifully supplied with arms and ammunition, the more warlike in appearance for a couple of field-pieces, and furnished with waggons and horses, tents, supplies of food, and every other necessity of a campaign. A white or blue ribbon or piece of tape in the button-hole, was the badge adopted in the districts near Lawrence. In the northern districts, the piece of hemp was the more customary mark of those who were ready to use the halter in proof of the soundness of their views. " Neither give nor take quarter," and " All right on the hemp," were their two pass-words.

As the number of illegal votes recorded by non-residents was 4,908, it may be estimated that this invading army numbered about five thousand men. The number of votes legally given, was 1,410 ; of which about 800 were given to the Free-state candidates. General David R. Atchison, recently Vice-president of the United States, announced at a convention held a short time previously, that there were 1,100 coming from his own county of Platte in Missouri ; and "if that wasn't enough, they could bring 5,000 more ; that they came to vote, and would vote, or kill every —— Abolitionist in the Territory."

Of course they conquered. The legal voters were for the most part driven away. Where they could not stuff the ballot-box, they stole it. Where the authorized election judges were strict in the performance of their duty, they held a pistol at their heads till they resigned, when they elected judges *impromptu* from their own number. All the fraud and brutality of the former election were re-enacted, only with more undisguised shamelessness and daring violence.

The testimony obtained by the Committee of Investigation, is very full with relation to this election. There is little room for choice in selecting from the report of the Commissioners one or other of the districts as an example of the account they have to tell. For shortness, I will extract the report of the Doniphan precinct in the 14th district, as a fair sample of the less violent of these electioneering specimens :—

"The evening before the election some 200 or more Missourians from Platte, Buchanan, Saline, and Clay counties, Missouri, came into this precinct, with tents, music, waggons, and provisions, and armed with guns, rifles, pistols, and bowie-knives, and camped about two miles from the place of voting. They said they came to vote, to make Kansas a slave state, and intended to return to Missouri after they had voted. On the morning of the election, the judges appointed by the governor would not serve, and others were chosen by the crowd.

" The Missourians were allowed to vote without being sworn, some of them voting as many as eight or nine times; changing their hats and coats, and giving in different names each time. After they had voted they returned to Missouri. The Free-state men generally did not vote, though constituting a majority in the precinct. Upon counting the ballots in the box, and the names on the poll-lists, it was found that there were too many ballots, and one of the judges of election took out ballots enough to make the two numbers correspond."

A carefulness so praiseworthy, that the ballots should not exceed in number the aggregate of the names on the poll-lists, does not appear to have been practised elsewhere. It is legitimate to infer this, from the fact, that whilst the whole number of persons in the Territory possessing a vote, according to the census taken the previous month, was only 2,905, the number of votes recorded on the Pro-slavery side alone was 5,427. Of this number, probably 530 were cast by residents. For every one legal vote, consequently, nine

illegal votes were given.   On the other hand
the Free-state candidates received 791 votes,
notwithstanding the intimidation which in
some districts entirely prevented the Free-
state men from exercising their rights.

This election was the occasion of bringing
into prominence one whose name has since
been an important one in Kansas annals,—
Sheriff Jones.   This Samuel Jones, at that time
post-master in Westport, Missouri, had the
command of the five or six hundred Missourians who were charged with the attack on the
polls in the second district.   The voting took
place at Bloomington, a place chiefly inhabited
by Free-state men, situated on the Wakarusa
Creek, about twelve miles above Lawrence.
The judges appointed by the Governor were
Messrs. Burson, Ramsay, and Ellison, by whom
the polls were opened in a log-house.   The
notable Jones, approaching the window of the
log-house, demanded for his Missourian cohort,
that they should be permitted to vote without
being sworn as residents of Kansas.   This was
refused.   The invading forces were then formed into small bands, and got ready their arms,

of which they had brought in ox-waggons an ample store.

"They again demanded," the Congressional Committee reports, " that the judges should resign; and, upon their refusing to do so, smashed in the window, sash and all, and presented their pistols and guns to them, threatening to shoot them. Some one on the outside cried out to them not to shoot, as there were Pro-slavery men in the house with the judges. They, then, put a pry under the corner of the house, and lifted it up a few inches, and let it fall again, but desisted upon being told there were Pro-slavery men in the house. During this time the crowd repeatedly demanded to be allowed to vote without being sworn, and Mr. Ellison, one of the judges, expressed himself willing, but the other two judges refused. Thereupon, a body of men, headed by Sheriff Jones, rushed into the judges' room with cocked pistols and drawn bowie-knives in their hands, and approached Burson and Ramsay. Jones pulled out his watch, and said he would give them five minutes to resign in, or die. When the five minutes had expired, and the judges did not resign, Jones said he would give them another minute and no more. Ellison told his associates that, if they did not resign, there would be one hundred shots fired in the room in less than fifteen minutes; and then, snatching up the ballot-box, ran out into the crowd, holding up the ballot-box and hurrahing for Missouri." This was followed by a complete row. The chief events were, the removal of the poll-books by Mr. Burson, the capture of the said books by Jones, the choice of two new judges, and the final and signal triumph of Sheriff Jones and his cohort of Missourians, in the proportion of more than ten illegal to one legal vote. The incident which occurred on this occasion to one of the residents of the district, Mr. Mace, I have already in a former chapter narrated.

A Presbyterian clergyman, the Rev Frederick Starr, who was an eye-witness of the fraud and intimidation practised at Leavenworth city, and has published a statement of this and preceding events, describes a scene by no means rare on the occasion of this election. " Some four days later," he writes, " I was on

my horse, returning from Platte city to Weston, when four waggons came along, and on the
bottom sat six men. A pole, about five feet
high, stuck upright at the front of the waggon; on its stop stuck an inverted empty
whisky-bottle; across the stick at right angles
was tied a bowie-knife; a black cambric flag,
with a death's-head and bones daubed on in
white paint, and a long streamer of beautiful
glossy Missouri hemp floated from the pole;
there was a revolver lashed across the pole,
and a powder-horn hanging loosely by it.
They bore the piratical symbols of Missouri
ruffians returning from Kansas." The clergyman then describes his surprise at being salut-
ed by the driver of the waggon as a friend.
Begrimed with dirt and with an eight or nine
days' absence from home, he scarcely knew
him. But the hand was held out, and to his
pain he had to recognize a gentleman well-
known and much respected in Platte City, belonging to the legal profession, son of a distinguished physician, " the most gentlemanly
and talented Southerner whom he ever met in
the South," with whom, moreover, he had

been associated two months previously in can-
vassing the county in favour of a Maine Liquor
Law. He was the captain of his party; they
numbered over forty in all; they had been to
vote at Fort Riley, the most distant of the
electoral districts, and had had a journey,
therefore, of nearly three hundred miles; they
"had had a good time." The clergyman went
his way, "wondering how education, custom,
interest, and sin could blind the eyes of God-
like intellect, and turn to stone the noblest
and most generous hearts."

Thus was elected the famous Legislature of
Kansas, which has since given laws to the territory, received the sanction of the Federal
Government, become the fountain-head of
legislative authority, and, backed by United
States troops, had ridden rough-shod over the
liberties and guaranteed privileges of the people, by perverting its power to the legalization
of the darkest injustice and oppression.

The returns from six of the districts were set
aside by Governor Reeder, on account of manifest illegality, and the elections consequently
in these districts were not confirmed. Had

more than four days been allowed for protest-
ing against the validity of the returns, and had
all persons who might venture so to protest not
been threatened with immediate hanging, it is
reasonable to suppose that the Governor would
have had to deal with other districts in like
manner.   Failing information, however, he
was compelled to grant certificates of election.
For the six districts disputed, he ordered new
elections for May 22nd.   " This infernal scoundrel will have to be hemped yet," writes the
editor of one of the Missouri journals, in com-
menting upon this act of the Governor.   In
one of the contested districts, Leavenworth,
the Missourian forces again carried the poll by
violence, on the occasion of the new election.
In the others, the Free-state settlers alone
voted, and of course returned their own candidates.

In the mean time Governor Reeder,—who was
far too independent, as well as too honourable
a man, to become the pliant tool of the Pro-
slavery party,—became increasingly unpopular
amongst his democratic friends.   Threats of
assassination were frequent, if he should dare

to refuse his confirmation of the illegal elections. Meetings were held, at which he was declared unfit to be Governor. One or two small attempts were made to elect a Governor in his place, whilst secret plots more efficacious in their nature were laid, by which to bring about his removal.

The fraudulent election of March 30th left the two parties in Kansas more widely sundered than before. The Free-state people were exasperated through finding themselves mercilessly trampled upon without a chance of redress. The advocates of slavery made no secret of what they had done: and, as the Missouri journals of that date abundantly show, openly exulted in the triumph Missouri had gained for slavery in Kansas. One newspaper, *The Parkville Luminary*, itself an advocate of Pro-slavery principles, yet venturing to demur to the interference of Missouri in the elections of Kansas, was branded as abolitionist and incendiary; and on the 14th April, an armed mob came down from Platte City, to inflict summary punishment. They destroyed the press and type, throwing them into the river, and seized upon the editor, who escaped being lynched only through his wife refusing to be severed from him.

The illegal Legislature, being now invested with power, proceeded to organize itself, and to commence the exercise of its authority. It assembled, therefore, as ordered by the Governor, at Pawnee, the highest settlement up the Kaw river, close to Fort Riley, and commenced its sittings on the 2nd July. One of the prime movers in the Missourian outrage, the Rev. Thomas Johnson of the Shawnee Mission, was elected President of the Council. The Speakership of the lower house was given to Dr. J. H. Stringfellow. There was one Free-state man in the Council, Mr. Conway. The legislature arranged that matter by expelling him, and giving his seat to his Pro-slavery opponent in the election. There remained one white sheep in the House of Representatives, Mr. Houston, returned by the settlers about Big Blue. That gentleman resigned his seat, having no wish to act in a Legislature illegally constituted. The five Free-state members who claimed their seats in consequence of the new election ordered by the Governor in the contested districts, were excluded, the Legislature ruling that they were the wrong members, and that the Pro-slavery men were the right, to whom accordingly their places were given. Thus was the Kansas Legislature purged of all opposing elements.

Elected by Missourian votes, and composed almost exclusively of residents of that State, notwithstanding that the law requires the delegates to be residents of Kansas, the Legislative Assembly sat during the months of July and August, 1855. For the sake of being nearer their home, they removed early in July, in spite of the veto of the Governor, to Shawnee Mission, on the border line of Missouri. There they legislated by day, and at Westport, in Missouri, two miles distant, they carried on their drunken revels at night.

Being in haste to give a code of laws to Kansas, they transferred into a volume of more than a thousand pages, the greater part of the laws of their own State, substituting the words "Territory of Kansas" for "State of Missouri." In protection of slavery, they enacted far more

rigorous laws than obtain in Missouri, or than
were ever before conceived of, making it a
felony to utter a word against the institution,
or even to have in possession a book or paper
which denies the right to hold slaves in Kansas. Some of these laws have already been
quoted in this volume. It will have been seen
that for every copy of a Free-state newspaper
which a person might innocently purchase, the
law would justify that person's condemnation
to penal servitude for two or five years, drag-
ging a heavy ball and chain at his ancle, and
hired out for labour on the public roads, or for
the service of private individuals, at the fixed
price of fifty cents per diem. So comprehen-
sive did these legislators make their slave code,
that by the authority they thus gave themselves, they could, in a very short time, have
made every Free-state man in the territory a
chained convict, standing side by side, if they
so pleased, with their slaves, and giving years
of forced labour for the behoof of their Pro-
slavery fellow-citizens.

The Legislature proceeded also to appoint
officers for the Territory. Even the executive

and judiciary were made to hold office from itself; and a Board of Commissioners chosen by
the Legislature, instead of the inhabitants
themselves, was empowered to appoint the
sheriffs, justices of the peace, constables, and
all other officers in the various counties into
which the territory was divided.

Every member of succeeding Legislatures,
every judge of election, every voter, must
swear to his faithfulness on the test-questions
of slavery. Every officer in the territory,
judicial, executive, or legislative, every attorney admitted to practise in the courts, every
juryman weighing evidence on the rights of
slaveholders, must attest his soundness in the
interest of slavery, and his readiness to endorse
its most repugnant measures.

For further security, the members of the
Assembly submitted their enactments to the
Chief Justice for confirmation. This judicial
confirmation was gratefully given; all they
had done was declared legal. And the sheriffs
and other local officers appointed by the Legislature, were equally ready with their aid in the
execution of these unjust laws.

There was a wonderful reciprocity in all this. Still more will this be evident, on the perusal of the hundred and forty pages of acts of incorporation, passed by the Legislative Assembly, by virtue of which joint-stock companies are called into being, and charters given to railway, mining, insurance, land-holding and other companies, to toll-bridges, ferries, plank-roads, even universities, beyond all that the territory can require for many years to come. In these public trusts, the champions of the Pro-slavery cause have a monopoly of power for years conferred upon them. And, whilst the members of the Legislature have more than amply repaid themselves, they have also, by a judicious introduction of other names into their grants, bound to themselves four or five hundred individuals, who, as favoured grantees, have become interested in upholding those laws upon the legality of which their grants depend.

CHAPTER XXII.

Removal of Governor Reeder.—Appointment of Governor Shannon.—Character of the two Governors contrasted.—Shannon's Declaration of Political Views.—Organization of the Free-state Party.—Independent Action to form a State Government.—Public Sentiment among the Southern Party. —Outrages.—A Clergyman floated on the Missouri.—Murder.—Slackness of the Law.—Singular Use of Judicial Power.

In consequence of the removal of the Houses of Legislature from the place he had designated as the capital, Governor Reeder declared their proceedings irregular and void. This heightened the enmity his impartial and cautious conduct had already aroused against him. He had been many times threatened with hanging, shooting, stabbing, and other forms of death; and he had been knocked down and kicked by General Stringfellow, while sitting in his office, and without having offered any offence. His removal, however, was essential to the success of the Missourian party. To effect this, there-

fore, they had used their influence with the
federal Government; and, on a charge of some
purchasers of land from the Kaw Indians, in
the matter of which he appears to have been
perfectly innocent, Andrew Reeder was, in the
month of July, 1855, removed by President
Pierce from the governorship of Kansas.

Reeder's successor in office was Wilson Shannon, who arrived in the territory on the 1st of
September.   In their new governor, the slavery
party had a man after their own heart.   He
had formerly been governor of Ohio, and had
held other high positions.   But he had also
seen rough life, and learned rough practices, in
California and Mexico ; and it would be difficult to conceive of a man more undignified in
his whole conduct, or more ill-fitted by natural qualifications for the responsibilities attach-
ing to a country's rule.

Shannon was the direct contrast to Reeder,
as well adapted to satisfy the wishes of the
Missourians, as his predecessor was the reverse.
Reeder was so firm in purpose and in act, that
it was vain to seek to turn him from his own
convictions.   " Gentlemen," he said on one

occasion, when, shortly after the election of
March, he was waited upon by a Pro-slavery
deputation, who informed him that he must
grant their candidates certificates of election or
die—"Gentlemen, two or three of you can
assassinate me, but a legion cannot compel me
to do that which my conscience does not ap-
prove." Shannon, on the other hand, was so
weak and pliable in the hands of those to whom
he had surrendered himself, that they could shape
his conduct perfectly at will. The first governor
of Kansas, notwithstanding that he came as
a man of the administration, was remarkable
for his moderation and impartiality ; he wished
apparently to put into practice the principle
of squatter sovereignty, according to the pure
and perfect ideal in which it had theoretically
presented itself to him. The second governor
saw in squatter sovereignty only another word
for the domination of the slave power,—never
so much as attempted to be moderate or impartial, and was prepared for the darkest tyranny
that ever disgraced human rule. Reeder was
ever reticent, and cautious of committing himself. Shannon was open and free; came

committed, and never intended it should be otherwise. The first declined the invitations made to him when he assumed office in the territory, and thereby saved his independence, as well as kept himself sober, although from that moment he fell in Missourian esteem. The second governor of Kansas accepted the hospitalities and convivialities of the Missourians in Westport the night before he entered the territory, displayed that love of good cheer which seems never to forsake him, and in the course of his speeches defined his intended policy in Kansas, with a point and plainness of speech which left his Missourian entertainers nothing to desire. "The enactments of *your* Legislature," he said, addressing the people of Missouri, " are valid, and I have the will, and am clothed with the power, to employ whatever force is necessary to carry them into execution; and I call upon *you* (again, the people of Missouri), to sustain me in the discharge of this duty." " As to slavery," writes the *Missouri Democrat* in reporting his speech, " he had no intention, he said, of changing his political faith ; he thought, with reference to

slavery, that as Missouri and Kansas were adjoining States, it would be well if their institutions should harmonize, otherwise there
would be continual quarrels and border feuds.
He was for slavery in Kansas. (Loud cheers.)"

During the same month in which Governor
Shannon commenced his administration, the
Free-state party, as an independent political
body, was organized. From their new governor the Free-state people saw that they had
nothing but high-handed oppression to expect ;
to the Federal power which they had memori-
alized in the hope of obtaining justice, they
looked in vain for redress; the law of the
territory defined their opinions as felonious, at
least if put into language, and condemned their
acts as rebellious and treasonable. They,
therefore, held their mass-meetings and con-
ventions, passed resolutions without number,
and, treating the fraudulent Legislature as spurious and consequently unpossessed of legislative authority, they availed themselves of the
right of American citizens to assemble together
in a peaceable manner to make provision for
their own government. Thus was set on foot

the Free-state organization, which, whether constitutional or otherwise in its mode of action, has brought itself into competition with the territorial authority, and given rise to the double governorship, double judiciary, double legislature, double militia, and in general, double claim to obedience, which has constituted so peculiar a feature in the politics of Kansas.

The Territorial Legislature had appointed Oct. 1, for the election of the delegate to Congress. The Free-state party, repudiating the acts of the Legislature, appointed Oct. 9 for the same purpose. General Whitfield, as before, was elected on the one occasion, Missourians again having the chief share in the polling. Andrew Reeder, the late Governor, was elected on the other, by a large vote from tbe Free-state population. The two candidates were sent, therefore, to Washington, to contest the seat. Delegates were also chosen to represent the Free-state people in Kansas at a convention for the purpose of framing a constitution. This convention met at Topeka between Oct. 23 and Nov. 11, and framed a constitution embodying Free-state views, under which appli cation was made to Congress for the admission of Kansas into the confederacy as a State. In the following month the people voted upon and adopted this constitution ; in January, 1856, they elected their Governor and other State officers, as well as a Senate and House of Representatives; on March 4, the State Government was organized, and the Legislature met to adopt a memorial to the Federal Government, and to adjourn till July ; and at the same time they received the President's special message and subsequent proclamation, in which their movement was denounced as rebellion, and power was granted to Governor Shannon to employ the United States troops for the suppression of every movement which placed itself in opposition to the Territorial Legislature, although that Legislature owed its existence to force and fraud.

Thus far the history of the efforts of the Free-state party to organize a State Government, in relating which I have anticipated by a little the narrative of the course of events generally in the Territory.

Possessing a code of laws which would jus-

tify the extermination of every Free-soiler in
the Territory, and having obtained in Wilson
Shannon a Governor ready from the heart to
execute those laws, the Slavery party had little
to interrupt its designs. The vow was often
expressed that " Missouri river should run red
with the blood of Abolitionists." The *Squatter Sovereign* uttered the feeling of the Southern party in words that admit of no second
meaning :—

" It is silly to suppose for an instant that
there can be peace in Kansas as long as one
enemy of the South lives upon her soil, or one
single specimen of an Abolitionist treads in the
sunlight of Kansas territory."

Again, the editor of the same organ waxes
yet warmer :—

" We are determined to repel this Northern
invasion, and make Kansas a Slave State ;
though our rivers should be covered with the
blood of their victims, and the carcasses of the
Abolitionists should be so numerous in the territory as to breed disease and sickness, we will
not be deterred from our purpose."

During the autumn of 1855, many enormities were committed by the warm adherents of slavery. But none probably was more revoltingly cruel than their treatment of a Western preacher, the Rev. Pardee Butler. This gentleman unfortunately set foot in the violently Pro-slavery town of Atchison. His sentiments were known, and for the purpose of proving them, and obtaining a pretext for the intended assault, a number of the "most respectable citizens" requested his signature to some Pro-slavery resolutions. He declined to give it. This was his crime. He was hurried away to the river, painted, lashed to some logs, and floated down the rapid tide.

But let the editor of the *Squatter Sovereign* tell the tale in his own words, for he was no passive spectator of the scene, and his own account of what his own hands took part in doing, will assuredly not err on the side of exaggeration.

"After the various plans for his disposal had been considered, it was finally decided to place him on a raft, composed of two logs firmly lashed together ; that his baggage and a loaf of bread be given him ; and, having attached a flag to his primitive bark, emblazoned with mottoes indicative of our contempt for such characters, Mr. Butler was set adrift on the great Missouri, with the letter R legibly painted on his forehead.

"He was escorted some distance down the river by several of our citizens, who, seeing him pass several rack-heaps in quite a skilful manner, bade him adieu and returned to Atchison.

"Such treatment may be expected by all scoundrels visiting our town for the purpose of interfering with our time-honoured institutions, and the same punishment we will be happy to award all Freesoilers, Abolitionists, and other emissaries."

Thus was a minister of the Gospel treated, against whom no heavier charge could be alleged, than that his opinions were not favourable to the extension of slavery. Mr. Butler fortunately escaped with his life, and from his own account we learn that the following were some of the mottoes emblazoned on his flag:—"The way they are served in Kansas." "Cargo insured,—unavoidable danger of the Missourians and the Missouri river excepted."

" Let future emissaries from the North beware. Our hemp crop is sufficient to reward all such scoundrels."

Two months later, Mr. Collins, who owned a saw-mill at Doniphan, was shot on similar political grounds, by a violent Pro-slavery man, named Patrick Laughlin. Pat came, it is said, originally from Ireland, and had rendered himself famous by an exposure, as it was termed, of the Kansas Legion. Laughlin was aided in this attack by three or four armed associates, and Mr. Collins' sons were present, and sought to defend their father. There was a considerable interchange of bowie-knife cuts and pistol-firing on this occasion, and the murderer himself was wounded. But the victim being a Free-state man, the law took no cognizance of the murder, and Laughlin found protection, and was rewarded by a situation in a shop in Atchison.

This reference to the slackness of the law suggests the remark that, through the whole course of the Kansas struggle, the idea of holding office for the administration of justice seems never to have entered the minds of those holding the legal appointments in the territory. They were appointed—whether judges, marshals, sheriffs, or constables—by a certain party which through fraud had got into power, for the extermination of the other party. The power of arrest, the power of imprisonment, the power of hanging, was theirs only that they might arrest, imprison, or hang Free-state men. Hence, murderers, if they have only murdered in behalf of slavery, have gone unpunished; whilst hundreds have been made to suffer for no other crime than the suspicion of entertaining Free-state sentiments.

CHAPTER XXIII.

Murder of Dow.—The Guilty acquitted, the Innocent arrested.
—The Midnight Rescue.—Rally to Arms.—The Wakarusa
War.—Position of the Encampments.—First Siege of Lawrence.—Its Defence.—Amusing Incidents.—Mournful Events.
—The Treaty of Lawrence.—Peace Festivities.—Disbanding
of the Ruffian Forces.—Discontent.—Barbarous Treatment
of Prisoners.—Murder of Mr. Brown.—Fiendish Cruelty.

Iᴛ was in the month of November, however,
that the great outburst of legalized violence
commenced, since which time the rule of
bloodshed and crime has not ceased. On the
21st of that month, in open day, a Pro-slavery
man named Coleman, living at Hickory Point,
shot dead his Free-state neighbour, Dow, as he
passed his cabin door. Dow's body lay in the
road, where it fell, till night, when Branson, at
whose house Dow boarded, carried it home.
The Free-state men were naturally indignant
at the murder, and held a meeting on the subject. Coleman, being alarmed, fled to the Gov-

ernor. His murder being on the right side, his act was politically a work of merit. The Free-state men, however, followed him, and insisted on his arrest. The anthorities refused either to issue a warrant, or to examine the murderer. On the other hand, Jones, the Sheriff, obtained a warrant for the arrest of Branson, whose only offence was that he had shown respect to the dead body of Dow. Summoning a posse of about twenty-five men, including two who were parties to the murder of the morning, Jones rode across to the scene of the murder, and reaching it at night, entered the cabin of the unoffending Branson. Finding him in bed, the sheriff drew his pistol, cocked it, and holding it at Branson's breast, said, " You are my pris-oner, and if you move I will blow you through." The other men cocked their guns, and gathering around Branson, took him prisoner. As they were riding off with their prisoner, some Free-state men who had heard of the deed, came up to the party and rescued Branson, without, however, shedding blood.

This transaction gave rise to what is known in Kansas as the " Wakarusa War." Jones, immediately after the rescue of Branson, wrote to Governor Shannon that an open rebellion had commenced on the part of the Free-state men, that he had been forcibly interfered with in the discharge of his duties, and that he expected the Governor to furnish him with a force of three thousand men, to aid him in the execution of the law. The Governor then issued a proclamation, calling on all to rally to arms in order to suppress the rising rebellion. He wrote to Richardson, Eastin, and Strickler, Generals of the new Territorial Militia, to collect all the forces they could command, and to place them at Sheriff Jones' disposal; whilst all the border-counties of Missouri were canvassed and taxed to supply men and arms for the new campaign.

The town of Lawrence, which had no share in the rescue of Branson, and whose only offence was that it was inhabited for the most part by Free-state people, was declared by the Governor to be in insurrection. By the Governor's own admission, not a single warrant was in the hand of any officer against any one of the citizens of Lawrence. But as the main object was to " wipe out the Yankee city," the forces that were enrolled were gathered at different points around Lawrence. In this manner an encampment was formed on the west, at Lecompton ; a second, under General Atchison's command, toward the north, on the opposite side of the river ; but the principal encampment was that on the eastern side, below Franklin, on the Wakarusa Creek, which has given its name to the campaign.

From Franklin, which stands upon the edge of the prairie-level, a grassy slope descends towards the stream, from which it is separated by the thick belting of timber which skirts the creek. In this bottom and timber-land, the lawless forces were herded, as day by day they came in succession from the Missouri border-towns. All passers-by were arrested, so that Lawrence was shut off from communication with the east. Acts of assault were numerous ; drunkenness was universal and incessant. They possessed cannon, rifles, powder, and ammunition of every kind, some of which had been forcibly taken by order of one of the judges from the United States arsenal at Liberty, in

Missouri. "These men," as Governor Shannon subsequently stated, "came to the Wakarusa camp to fight; they did not ask peace; it was war—war to the knife." In another statement, referring to this rabble host, the Governor says with enthusiasm, "Missouri sent not only her young men, but her gray-headed citizens were there; the man of seventy winters stood shoulder to shoulder with the youth of sixteen." In all, Governor Shannon admits that there were as many as fifteen hundred men under arms, collected by the 1st or 2nd December. They continued to flow in after that date, and only waited until they felt themselves sufficiently strong in number, to make the longed-for attack upon Lawrence.

Within Lawrence, arming, drilling, fortifying, meeting-holding, and resolution-passing, went on continually amongst its Free-state inhabitants. Dr. Robinson was appointed Commander-in-Chief, and urged ever moderation and caution; General Lane, his associate in command, inspirited his soldiers, and prepared them to stand boldly at the expected blow. Many strange incidents occurred during this anxious time.

Some were curious, as, for example, the conveyance of the brass howitzer from Kansas City in a box, in the course of which, being "stalled down" in ascending from the ford, a party of border-ruffians, who stopped to question, were induced by the Yankee-driver of the team to help him out of his difficulty, and to forego their examination of his questionable merchandize. No less amusing was the stratagem of two intrepid Lawrence ladies, who, in order to replenish the supplies of gunpowder and rifle-caps, found space for two kegs of the former, and a quantity of caps and lead, beneath the wide circumference of their fashionable dresses, and walled round with combustible, safely passed the ruffian patrol, and reached the city with their precious charge.

But other events were of a sadly different character. Most mournful of all was the shooting of poor Thomas Barber, and the distracting grief of his widow. For no fault of his own, except that he was on the road when General Richardson, Judge Cato, Judge Wood, Colonel Burns, Major Clarke, and some others were passing, he was shot. Burns and Clarke were the two by whom the death-stroke was given, for they both shot him ; but as he continued to keep his saddle for some minutes, the others, judges and generals as they were, joined in the pursuit of his two companions and the sinking body, until one of these, the brother of poor Barber, unable longer to sustain the lifeless corpse, left it on the road, and the two, pressing forward their horses, saved their lives by flight.   And who was to arrest the murderers ? No one.   A judge of the Supreme Court, holding office by Federal appointment, was of the party, an approving spectator, if not an actor in the outrage.   Higher legal sanction could not be given.

Fortunately for humanity, Governor Shannon, who is almost as weak as he is tyrannical, became frightened of the lawless host he had collected around Lawrence, and finding Colonel Sumner unwilling to aid him without definite instructions from the Government, he concluded a treaty of peace with the leaders of the Free-state party.   This was on Sunday, the 9th December, twelve days after the issue of his proclamation of war.   The treaty was signed

at Lawrence by Governor Shannon on the one
hand, and Generals Robinson and Lane on the
other. The following day, the people of Lawrence invited their late besiegers to a supper
and dance, and celebrated the pacification by
joyous festivities. The Governor, however,
did not wait for these convivialities. To show
how true his heart was, and how friendly his
feelings, he drank the health of every Free-state
man that came into the Cincinnati House. As
he went his way, with Jones and others as an
escort, he is reported by Mr. Phillips the correspondent of the New York *Tribune*, to have
explained how his character was misapprehended by the people of Lawrence. " Now,
ge—entlemen, you—hic—you don't understand
me. You all abuse me, but—hic—but it's be—
because you don't know me. Get to know
me right—hic—well, and you'll—hic—you'll
find I'm a—hic—I'm a h—ll of a fellow."

The news of the pacification was received
with much indignation by the rabble forces
collected at the Wakarusa camp. Governor
Shannon was accused of having played false,
and many talked of lynching him. However,

the orders came from the Governor to disband
the forces, and neither Atchison nor Stringfellow durst lead them on to the attack of Law
rence, much as they wished it, when not
shielded by the territorial authority. Above
all, the whiskey was, as the Western men say,
" a'most gi'n out"—a circumstance which was
of itself sufficient to cause the abandonment of
the enterprise; and the cold had become so
intense, that even their great camp-fires scarcely
sufficed to make the exposure endurable. The
consequence was that the camp on the Wakarusa was broken up; the forces retired in like
manner from Lecompton and the left bank of
the Kaw; and the first campaign in Kansas had
reached its termination.

To those accustomed to more settled methods
of government, it may seem incomprehensible
that a town should be surrounded by a besieging army, and should have more than fifteen
hundred men placed under arms against it
by the ruling power, when no crime had been
committed against the State by any of its
inhabitants, when not a single legal warrant
was in existence against any of the people, and

when they testified their readiness to give up to the proper officers any person against whom such warrants might be issued. Yet such was the position of Lawrence. The Committee of Investigation, after fully weighing all the testimony upon the subject, reported that they could see " no reason, excuse, or palliation" for the feeling of hostility evinced in this invasion of Lawrence.

Of the gross cruelty which was practised against those of the Free-state men who fell into the hands of the officers of the territory, it may suffice to present one example out of many—that relating to the arrest of Dr. Cutler and Mr. Warren. I have heard very full accounts of this transaction, but prefer giving it in the words of the Congressional Committee :—

"They were taken without cause or warrant, sixty miles from Lawrence, and when Dr. Cutler was quite sick.* They were compelled

* The place of arrest was in the neighbourhood of Doniphan, where Dr. Cutler resided. He was returning home after a severe illness, from which he had endeavored to recruit himself by a stay at Dr. Robinson's house in Lawrence.

to go to the camp at Lecompton, and were put into the custody of Sheriff Jones, who had no process to arrest them. They were taken into a small room, kept as a liquor-shop, which was open and very cold. That night Jones came in with others, and went to 'playing poker at twenty-five cents ante.' The prisoners were obliged to sit up all night, as there was no room to lie down when the men were playing. Jones insulted them frequently, and told one of them he must either 'tell or swing.' The guard then objected to this treatment of prisoners, and Jones desisted. G. F. Warren thus describes their subsequent conduct: 'They then carried us down to their camp. Kelly, of the *Squatter Sovereign*, who lives in Atchison, came round and said he thirsted for blood, and said he should like to hang us on the first tree. Cutler was very weak, and that excited him so that he became delirious. They sent for three doctors, who came. Dr. Stringfellow was one of them. They remained there with Cutler until after midnight, and then took him up to the office, as it was very cold in camp.' "

Of the many acts of infamy which occurred during the short interval between the termination of the Wakarusa War and the opening of

the second campaign already described in the
early chapters of this volume, I will only refer
to one, which occurred in January, 1856 ; this
was the murder of Mr. Brown, of Leavenworth.
Mr. Brown's offence was, that he had rescued a
Free-state man from the hands of a party of
ruffians who were about to take his life. Whilst
thus acting, a band of Kickapoo Rangers arrived,
armed as usual with their rifles and hatchets. A
fight of some hours' duration ensued, notwithstanding that it was night ; wounds were given
on both sides, and a Pro-slavery man, named
Cook, fell in the encounter. After this, Mr.
Brown, returning with seven others to Leavenworth, was again attacked by the company of
the Rangers, by whom they were taken prisoners and carried into a shop in Easton. There
some of the citizens of the place joined in the
outrage. The Captain of the Rangers did his
best for a time to protect Mr. Brown. At
length, however, he left him, when the crowd,
infuriated by liquor, surrounded their victim,
and taking their hatchets literally hacked him
to death. The wound of which he died was a
deep hatchet-gash on the side of the head, in-

flicted by a man named Gibson. Poor Brown lingered long enough after the fatal blow to suffer yet more exquisite refinements of cruelty, whilst the ruthless savages kicked him, jumped upon his fallen body, spat tobacco-juice into his eyes, and barbarously mutilated his body.

This murder was again on the right side of politics, and no attempt therefore was made to bring to justice the perpetrators of the foul deed. Many, however, are well known. Some were officers of the law; one of the most refined in cruelty has already been mentioned in these pages as the United States Deputy Marshal; and others were of "the most respectable" inhabitants of the place.

It is difficult to believe that, after acts of such enormity, the President declared in his message on Kansas, that "no acts prejudicial to good order have occurred under circumstances to justify the interposition of the federal government."

CHAPTER XXIV.

Change in Popular Feeling after the Destruction of Lawrence.
—Retaliation.—Massacre at Osawatomie.—Personal Experi-
ence.—Battles of Black Jack and Franklin.—Sack of Osa-
watomie.— Road-side Horrors.—Hanging. — Repulsion of
Northern Immigrants.—A Barbarous Wager.—Murder and
Scalping.—The Atrocity Completed.—August.—Murder of
Major Hoyt.—Burning of Pro-slavery Forts.—Colonel Titus
Seized and Liberated.—Treaty of Peace.—Militia Called
Out.—Proclamation of Rebellion.—" The Army of Law and
Order in Kansas Territory."—Second Fight at Osawato-
mie.—General Lane's Free-state Army.—Expulsion of the
Free-state Inhabitants of Leavenworth.—The President's
Messages.

THE events described in the preceding chapters
bring the history of the contest in Kansas
down to the spring of 1856. The still more
stirring events which succeeded have already
been described in the chapters of personal narrative, with which this volume commenced.
The later history of the territory claims a brief
notice.

The attack and burning of Lawrence wrought

a great change in popular feeling. Of this many evidences came under my own observation. " We will stand it no longer," was the substance of what I heard on every side from the Free-state adherents. Before I left, it had become the universal conviction, alike of the Pro-slavery and the Free-state party, that a civil war had fairly commenced; and this conviction was shared in even by those in authority. The territory was placed, not under martial law, but under territorial law maintained by the United States forces; and the well-mounted dragoons from Fort Leavenworth might be seen stationed at various points along the valley of the Kaw, to sustain the authority of the governor. At the same moment came the news from Washington of the outrage committed in the Senate chamber upon the person of Mr. Sumner. I well remember the effect this had upon many, who concluded that the rule of force and violence had been fairly inaugurated even in the highest places of the land, and was no longer restricted to the lawless inhabitants of the frontier. Bands of men under military command paraded the streets of Leavenworth; others guarded the points of egress from the city. They held lists in their hands, containing the names of Free-state men, whom they made rapid work of seizing and placing in confinement. The Committee of Investigation, although holding appointment from Congress, found itself compelled to interrupt its sittings. Every hour brought intelligence of some fresh deed of violence or wrong.

The exasperation, however, wrought in the minds of the Free-state men, led to many acts of retaliation. Convinced that a civil war had begun, they ceased in many places to hesitate, and boldly met the sword by the sword, violence by violence. The marauding bands of Pro-slavery men, who had been long scouring the country and committing inhuman outrages upon all who were politically obnoxious, were met by guerrilla parties on the Free-state side, whose repeating fire-arms frequently proved more than a match for the heavy, long-barrelled Mississippi guns of their opponents. At Osawatomie a horrible massacre took place, of which the actual circumstances will probably never be known. I was at Leavenworth when it happened; but as far as I could ascertain, a fight had occurred between half a dozen Pro-slavery men and as many or more of the opposite party. Every Pro-slavery man was left dead, as well as three of the Free-state men. At the time when this took place, the spirit which pervaded the minds of both parties in that district, was one of war even to extermination. As long as I remained in the Territory, outrages and bloodshed were of daily, frequently much more than daily occurrence. It were easy to fill many chapters with the details.

There was not unanimity, however, in the Free-state councils; for, whilst one portion engaged in open warfare, especially with a view to the recovery of stolen horses and other property, others* adhered to the last to their former policy of non-resistance, and held meetings, made speeches, and passed resolutions, condemnatory of the active measures of their brother Free-state men.

Thus ended May, 1856, and June came in with a continuance of the same measures of

---

* And much the larger portion, including all the original leaders of the Free-state party.—Am. Ed

hostility and frequent collision. On the 2nd of June occurred the battle of Black Jack, near Palmyra; on the night of the 4th occurred that of Franklin. Each of these terminated favourably to the Free-state men. On the 8th occurred the sack of Osawatomie; its offence, like that of Lawrence, being that it was inhabited by Free-state settlers. This abominable outrage was effected by some Missouri companies, which General Whitfield had organized, and was making use of in various parts south of the Kaw. Colonel Sumner was on the field, also, with his dragoons, during all the early part of June, endeavoring to restore order and prevent collisions. Why the attack was permitted, however, on the defenceless town of Osawatomie, does not appear.

On the road in the neighborhood of Westport and Kansas City, outrages were of daily occurrence at the time I left the Territory. Companies of armed plunderers, under Captain Pate and other leaders, used to camp out near the Lawrence road, and attack all Free-state men who might fall into their hands. One New England man, by name Barlow, they proceeded to hang on the bough of a tree as an Abolitionist, and, with the rope around his neck, raised him from the ground. But one of their number induced them to relent, having extorted from the poor man, who had settled in Lawrence, a promise that he would leave the Territory within twelve hours; and having also robbed him of his oxen, waggon, and goods. He, therefore, lived to tell the tale. But many were not so fortunate, and oftener than once or twice dead bodies were found dangling from the boughs of trees, or murdered and mutilated forms discovered by the bare road-side.

Towards the end of June, the Pro-slavery men adopted the system of stopping all the parties of emigrants from the free States, and, after robbing them, sending them back whence they came. In the following month, the passage through the State of Missouri was wholly interdicted to men of northern views; armed forces were stationed and batteries erected on the river-side; hence the only approach from the north was by a tedious route through Iowa and Nebraska.

Individual instances of barbarity continued to occur almost daily. In one instance, a man belonging to General Atchison's camp made a bet of six dollars against a pair of boots, that he would go out and return with an Abolitionist's scalp within two hours. He went forth on horseback. Before he had gone two miles from Leavenworth on the road to Lawrence, he met a Mr. Hops, driving a buggy. Mr. Hops was a gentleman of high respectability, who had come with his wife, a few days previously, to join her brother, the Rev. Mr. Nute, of Boston, who had for some time been labouring as a minister in Lawrence. The ruffian asked Mr. Hops where he came from. He replied, he was last from Lawrence. Enough! The ruffian drew his revolver and shot him through the head. As the body fell from the chaise, he dismounted, took his knife, scalped his victim, and then returned to Leavenworth, where, having won his boots, he paraded the streets with the bleeding scalp of the murdered man stuck upon a pole. This was on the 19th August of last year. Eight days later, when the widow, who had been left at Lawrence sick, was brought down by the Rev. Mr. Nute, in the hope of recovering the body of the murdered husband, the whole party, consisting of about twenty persons in five waggons, was seized, robbed of all they had, and placed in confinement. One was shot the next day for attempting to escape. The widow and one or two others were allowed to depart by steamer, but penniless. A German incautiously condemning the outrage, was shot; and another saved his life only by precipitate flight.

To narrate the history of these summer months, would be to present a succession of similar atrocities, committed under the name of law, and " with a view to maintain public order in the territory."

During the month of August alone, besides the brutal homicide just mentioned, there occurred another in which a company of Georgians, in their vengeance against Mayor Hoyt, fairly riddled his body with their bullets. This took place at a fort on Washington Creek, which was one of a number of military posts that had been erected in different parts, and garrisoned by southern bands. The murder led to retaliation. The Free-state men burned the fort, and the Georgians took to flight. They also attacked the post at Franklin, which, after a keen contest and some loss, was surrendered in like manner, the cannon and arms being left in the hands of the Free-state men. The next day, Colonel Titus's house near Lecompton, which was another of the southern head-quarters, was attacked, and after loss of life on both sides, Titus himself and eighteen others were taken prisoners. These acts of the Free-state party were those of men exasperated by the presence of murderous bands, who were daily putting into execution their threats of extermination, who did not hesitate at times to shoot their prisoners, and who were carrying on a ceaseless system of rapine and murder. Neither did the Free-state people thus resort to arms, until they had asked and been refused their personal protection at the hands of the federal troops, which were stationed in the neighbourhood for the ostensible purpose of preventing violence and restoring good order in the territory.

The successes of the Free-state party led

Governor Shannon to conclude a second treaty at Lawrence, which stipulated for peace, and led to an exchange of prisoners. No sooner had peace been made, however, than hostilities were resumed. The following day General Richardson had called out the militia to put down the Free-state men; and, three days later, the Governor proclaimed the territory to be in a state of insurrection, and rallied all to arms. General Atchison, who had been recruiting in Missouri, was advancing into the territory with 450 men. This number increased in a few day to 1,150 rank and file, a large proportion mounted, and well supplied with cannon and arms. The whole body was formed into two regiments under Generals Atchison and Reid, and assumed the name of "The Army of Law and Order in Kansas Territory." Plundering parties continued to commit almost incredible outrages. Fights occurred whenever opposing parties met. Atchison's army moved towards Osawatomie, and, before the month of August had expired, that small town had for a second time been subjected to a merciless attack. The disparity in number was overwhelming, and, after a hot contest of several hours, Captain Brown's little Free-state band was finally driven out from the wood in which they had sheltered themselves. The besiegers then burned a considerable portion of the town; but the loss on the side of the southern army was very large. Three waggon-loads of dead and wounded were removed from the place.

The presence of this southern army of extermination, which effectually blockaded the country east of Lawrence, and prevented supplies from reaching the Free-state settlements, called out General Lane from Lawrence, who again put the Free-state stronghold under defence, and organized forces by which he drove back the southern army to Missouri. Then ensued attack and repulse, victory and defeat, and all that chain of hostile events which have been rendered familiar to us by the accounts of the operations of the two conflicting armies. Leavenworth at this time became a scene of daily outrage. The Free-state residents—many of them merchants in the place, having valuable stocks of goods, and possessed of property besides—were literally driven out of the place, a hundred at a time, at the point of the bayonet, some escaping by the boats, others seeking refuge in the woods and ultimately at the fort. Their property fell for the most part into the hands of the administrators of "law and order;" and some who escaped by the river had not the means to pay their passage out of the scene of strife.

Thus commenced September, for I have only related the events of a single month, as an illustration of the wild anarchy and bloodthirsty fury which reigned throughout the summer of 1856. In view of these events, it is almost an insult to read the message of President Pierce upon the condition of Kansas. Mark how careful he is to sustain the authority of the party which assumed to be that of "law and order," and to guard against all infringement of the liberty to do wrong:—

"But it is not," he said in his first Special Message, "the duty of the President of the United States to volunteer interposition by force to preserve the purity of elections either in a State or Territory. To do so would be subversive of public freedom. And whether a law be wise or unwise, just or unjust, is not a question for him to judge. If it be constitutional—that is, if it be the law of the land—it is his duty to cause it to be executed, or to sustain the authorities of any State or Territory in executing it, in opposition to all insurrectionary movements."

President Pierce regarded the monstrous code of Kansas as constitutional, and therefore to be backed by his executive power, because it is, by the enactment of a false Legislature, the law of the Territory. Could he have forgotten, that no law is constitutional which violates the Constitution? Now, the Constitution of the United States guarantees every citizen liberty of speech; the laws of Kansas make speech in favour of freedom a punishable crime. The Constitution guarantees freedom of the press; the Kansas code forbids on pain of imprisonment the printing of so much as an "inuendo" that might be dangerous to slavery, and Kansas mobs, aided by federal troops, raze to the ground and burn to ashes Free-state printing-offices. The Constitution guarantees trial by jury for every accused person; the law of Kansas forbids

Free-state men to sit as jurors; and the idea of a jury is in practice treated as a nullity The Constitution guarantees liberty, and promises protection in the exercise of the electoral franchise; in Kansas every election that is recognized by the central Government, has been carried by rifle and revolver. The Constitution guarantees the sacredness of personal right, promises to guard the citizen's property, and to protect his liberty of person and of residence; in Kansas, men are driven by hundreds from their intended homes, robbed of their possessions, held in forced confinement, compelled to leave the land, for no crime but that of holding Free-state views, or that of being natives merely of northern soil.

And when a second and a third time the President was appealed to by the Free-state people in Kansas to exercise his power for the prevention of wrong, they only received the same cold answer. They were referred to the laws,—laws which condemned many of them to death, and all to imprisonment and penal labour. They were told to value the political blessings they enjoyed.

CHAPTER XXV.

Governor Geary.—His Pacific Proclamation.—Its Interpreta-
tion.—Release of State Prisoners on Bail.—Capture of
Ninety-eight Free-state Men.—Their Condition in Prison.—
Revolting Inhumanity towards the Prisoners.—Sufferings
of the Settlers.—Sickness, Cold, Hunger, and Orphanage.—
The Present and the Future of Kansas.—Action of Congress.

In the autumn of 1856, Wilson Shannon was
succeeded in the governorship of the territory
by its present Governor, John W. Geary.*　For
the Free-state inhabitants the change could not
be for the worse, such was the character of the
man from whose tyranny, and at the same time,
despicable weakness, they were thus relieved.
Some were led to hope for peace and protection; and many in this country may have
inferred from the apparently pacific tone of the
new Governor's proclamation, that a brighter

* Who resigned in March, 1857, and is succeeded by
Robert J. Walker.—Am. Ed.

day was at length dawning upon Kansas. Such anticipations have not, however, been realized. The Governor's pacific proclamation must be interpreted on the same principles with the President's pacific messages. He promised to quell insurrection; but the law defines as insurrectionary every organized action of the Free-state party. He promised to enforce laws; but law is only another name for oppression. He promised, if the people would obey, to restore peace, tranquillity, and order; but the price of that peace is a surrender to the slave power. And that he might make the people obey, he said he should feel justified in calling out the militia, employing the federal troops, and using the utmost firmness and authority in his power. And very much in accordance with his proclamation thus interpreted, the new Governor has acted

Dr. Robinson and his fellow-prisoners, who had been confined at Lecompton since the month of May, on a charge of usurpation of office and high treason, were indeed admitted to bail in the month of September, notwithstanding the strenuous attempt made to defer the case until April, when the prisoners would have been eleven months in confinement before their charge was brought up. The Free-state Legislature, which met in July, and was dispersed by Colonel Sumner at the head of the United States dragoons, endeavoured again to meet in the spring of the present year, but were prevented by the Governor. But would we know what spectacle Kansas has presented during the rigour of the past winter and under the present governorship, let the voices from the political prisons of Lecompton answer. I have before me an address to the American people, signed by ninety-eight Free-state men, who were then suffering a long and wretched imprisonment for their political offences.

After narrating at length the particulars of their capture, shortly after the arrival of Governor Geary, they proceed as follows :—

" We come now, at last, to speak of a subject too immediate, too vital, to admit of our passing it unnoticed, yet too full of horror to dwell upon. We allude to our treatment and condition since our confinement here, any description of which must come far short of the terrible reality. A few of our guard will ever be remembered by us with emotions of the deepest gratitude for their kindness ; but the greatest portion of them are drunken, brawling demons, too vile and wicked for portrayal. Times without number have they threatened to either shoot or stab us, and not unfrequently have they attempted to carry out their base and hellish threats. Several nights have the guard amused themselves throughout their different watches, by cursing us, throwing stones at the house, breaking in glass, sash, &c. Two large cannon stand planted but a few yards from our prison, and two nights has the match been swung several hours in the hands of the gunners, with orders to discharge both, heavily loaded with shot and slugs, upon us, in case our friends should come in sufficient force to avenge our wrongs. These, however, are only slight, compared with other insults and sufferings heaped upon us daily. Most of us are poorly clad—few have any bedding. Our prison is open and airy, yet small ; without, surrounded with unearthly filth; within, all is crawling with vermin, all, everything, mixed with misery. When youths, we listened with doubt to the dark stories of the Jersey prison-ships, and the Black-hole of Calcutta, never dreaming that we should at last be a sad, actual part of their

counterpart! More than once have we prophe-
sied to one another, that all would not leave
this charnel-house alive. Our assertions have
been verified; several have been dangerously
sick, one has died. His name was William
Bowles, and formerly from St. Charles, Mo.
He laboured with us nobly for our God-given
rights, and it was with feelings of unutterable
sorrow that we parted with him. After an
illness of two days, he left his sufferings this
morning, at one o'clock. Before his death, we
requested the officers of the guard to have him
removed to a place of quiet. We talked and
became tired, yet nothing was done. Last
night all the physicians in town were sent for,
and each refused to come. Dr. John P. Wood,
who is also judge of probate and committal justice, could not come, 'because he was sick;' yet
he was seen that evening, as well as the following morning, doing hard labour. Others had
reasons, we know not what. Dr. Brooks was
sent for five times; but as he was at a card-
table playing poker, he swore he 'would not
leave the game to save every —— Abolitionist
in the territory.'

"Sickness and death of the most horrid forms
are in our midst; the scrapings of Pandemo-
nium surround us; we can see nothing left us
but an appeal to the last tribunal, with God as

our judge, and our jury the great American people."

But it is not in the prison alone that the unoffending settlers of Kansas have had to endure fearful suffering. A gentleman from Chicago, who visited the territory in the winter on behalf of a committee of relief, whilst he confirmed the preceding statements, reported further that he found many of the settlers reduced by these acts of political oppression to the very verge of starvation. In one district he met with forty families entirely destitute, some of the fathers being confined in the Lecompton prison; their food green pumpkins and green Indian corn, grated by the hand. In another he found a family of five motherless children, the eldest only seven years old, in a state of starvation, their father a prisoner at Lecompton. In a third he discovered a hundred families, so destitute of clothing that they were ashamed to be seen. Again, a neighbourhood where nearly every person was sick; and another place where a family had subsisted for four weeks on nothing but wolves' meat. This gentleman visited all the settled portions of

Kansas, and everywhere he had visible proof that sickness and hunger had followed, as is usual, in the train of war.

Looking at the prospects of Kansas in the future, it affords some encouragement to know that the territory has been relieved of some few of those who were foremost in plotting strife and upholding the Reign of Terror. The present Governor has not permitted himself to be the tool of the border-ruffian leaders, in a like manner with his predecessor. Lecompte, "the Jeffreys of the territory," has been removed from the office of Chief Justice.* Colonel Titus, who with Buford commanded the southern bands from Georgia and other States, and filled the land when I was there with the terror of his deeds, has recently left the territory to join Walker in Nicaragua, and thus resume his former career as a filibusterer. Many besides, throughout the struggle, who have gone from the South to engage in the Kansas war, have become disgusted when they witnessed the

* It was so stated with authority at the close of Pierce's administration; but the rumor proved to be unfounded.—AM. ED.

reality, and have in a better spirit returned to their homes.

Nevertheless, peace is not yet in Kansas, and the question is not yet decided whether the new territory shall be an accession of soil to slavery or to freedom. Right has not yet taken the place of wrong, nor liberty been substituted for despotic oppression. At Washington there are indeed hopeful signs in relation to the action of the Federal Government. The Committee on Territories has presented to Congress a report, which recommends the repudiation of the acts of the Kansas Legislature as those of a spurious body, and the repeal of the whole Kansas code, which has given sanction to the bloodshed and crime under which the territory has groaned. This measure, which, if adopted, would be a first great step towards remedying the wrongs of Kansas, has obtained a majority in the House of Representatives. On the other hand, whilst these sheets have been passing through the press, the intelligence has arrived of the bill having been rejected in the Senate. How the contest will end, time alone can show.

CHAPTER XXVI.

SUPPLEMENT BY THE AMERICAN EDITOR.

APRIL 13, 1857.

ALL the federal offices in Kansas continue to
be filled by the ring-leaders of the conspiracy
against free-labor. Some of them are guilty
directly in their own persons, and all are guilty
indirectly, as conspirators and abettors, before
and after the fact, of the murder of citizens
whose only offense was a confession that they
preferred that slavery should not be established
in the territory. Let the reader not slight this
statement. It would be a disgraceful and
wicked thing for one to make such assertions
without adequate ground of perfect conviction
of their truth. If undeniable or if convincing
testimony of their truth is readily within his
reach, no man who respects himself, and who
would live with a clear conscience, can fail to
regard them gravely, anxiously, indignantly.

It is a simple, undeniable, indefensible fact, that the new President of the United States not merely still refrains from executing justice in Kansas, but also that he has renewed and extended the countenance, patronage, honors, and friendship of the government to men who regard it as a merit and a matter of boasting that, for a political purpose, they have shot, in cold blood, and in the back, citizens of several independent, sovereign free states, of whom they knew no harm but that they intended to vote against the establishment of slavery in territory belonging to those states, and of which they were residents and land-owners.

With a possible exception in the new secretary, there is no man now in Kansas recognized by our federal government, including its judicial branches, to have any official authority there, who is not a notorious plotter and probable pledged conspirator to prevent an honest action of the law of Squatter Sovereignty, as it is defined by the President and all its friends.

There are plenty of Free-state men from the North, capable and respectable, who have

always belonged to the Democratic party, and
who supported Mr. Buchanan in the hope that
he would be just to Kansas, but not one such has
been appointed to office.

The Hon. R. J. Walker has been selected
to succeed Governor Geary, who resigned his
office, either because, as his enemies say, he
considered his life in danger from the Pro-
slavery faction, or, as his friends say, because
the President refused to sustain him in taking
any measures inclining towards justice. Governor Walker has been recently known to the
public chiefly for his efforts to have a railroad
built from his state of Mississippi through a
district at present occupied chiefly by non-
slaveholding farmers in Texas, and thence a
thousand miles across a desert country to that
portion of California which is nearest to the
cotton-soils of Sonora, and which it is thought
might be made a slave state even without this
assistance. He asserts that he desires to have
the free-soil party in Kansas treated with fairness. He is the only one at present holding
office for Kansas, who has ever made this profession. He remains yet in Washington, attend-

ing to some necessary private business: he is a business man, and was a subscriber for one million dollars' worth of the stock of the Grand Southern California Railroad Company. Nevertheless, it is thought he may take a look at the territory in May.

Under a process of law, which the President recognizes as constitutional and valid, many good citizens, accused of resistance to the tyranny of an organization made by the Missourians for the purpose of establishing slavery in Kansas, have been torn from their families, and held in unwholesome confinement until some died and all were greatly impoverished. Of the many hundred boasting robbers and murderers of Free-state settlers, none yet are punished or even rebuked by the officers appointed to execute justice in the name of the majesty of the people of the confederate states.

The body of men who were last year appointed by the partisans of slavery for the purpose of preventing the success of any movements unfavorable to the establishment of slavery in the territory, and whose acts for that purpose are laws to the President of the

United States and all those whom he appoints
to office, have recently pretended that they
were willing to give an opportunity to the
people of the territory to indicate, by a vote,
what they demanded in their government. The
instrument of this pretension—just now warmly
commended by the Northern friends of Slavery
extension, because it is the first act of this
body which assumes to be intended to carry out
their petted principle of Squatter Sovereignty—
is the same which ex-Governor Geary vetoed on
the ground of the absurd inconsistency of its
provisions with its alleged purpose. It provides for a census of the citizens of the territory
who were resident in it, on the 15th March,
when no emigrants from the Free states would
be likely to have recently become resident, but
when, as it has now been made manifest, mul-
titudes would have just come in by land from
Missouri. From the census thus taken by offi-
cials, every one of whom is a sworn enemy of
freedom, a voting list is to be made up, which
is to be revised by sworn friends of slavery.
The territory is then to be formed into nineteen
voting districts, the size, and shape, and rela-

tions of which, to each other, and to Missouri, are to be determined by men who are ashamed of nothing which has been done to subdue the free-soil party of the territory in the last two years. The number of delegates who are to represent the people of each district, is to be proportionate to the population returned by the special census. This proportion, not very difficult for a business man to ascertain, is to be declared by the Governor and Secretary, appointed by the President, and as this is the only duty connected with the election assigned to the governor, it is evident that the " Legislature" had some misgivings that the friends of Mr. Buchanan, in the Free states, were speaking the truth when they declared that he was disposed to do the fair thing with Kansas.

Finally, the votes are to be taken, not by ballot, but *viva voce*, by vocal declaration, so that the slavery party may not be voted against by one man who is not willing to make himself known as a free-soiler to the land-officers, who are to settle disputed claims—and there are comparatively few claims which are not disputed—these land-officers being all men committed to, and identified with, the conspiracy, to establish slavery on the soil of Kansas. The inspectors of election are to be men similarly pledged or sworn to disregard the rights of the free-soilers, and by such trusty hands, the vote is to be recorded, and returned. The whole process, in short, is in the hands of the same unscrupulous miscreants, who have been protected in every crime of which the reader has read in this book, by the present federal judiciary. It has been often reported, of late, that the scandalous laws enacted last year by the Legislature, established by Missouri in the territory, have been repealed under the conciliatory policy of the session of this year. Certain laws which it would have been impracticable to attempt to execute, have been repealed. It yet remains a legal felony for any man in the territory to order a book, such as this, for instance, to be sent to him. Any one who offers to receive a free-soil newspaper, is liable to five years imprisonment. No conscientious free-soiler is eligible to sit upon a jury; and, in general, no practicable means of harassing, persecuting, and silencing, those who would act effectively against the establishment of slavery in the territory, are left unprovided for.

And, yet, it is very plainly declared by Governor Walker, after long consultation with the President, pending his acceptance of the governship, that he will attempt to carry out these laws, and force the people to accept this tyrannical usurpation of authority as a constitutional republican government. He believes, we are told, that it will be impossible to establish slavery in Kansas, because of its ungenial climate, (though it is milder than that of Virginia) therefore we are to believe that he will not lend himself to the schemes of his old friends, who have shrunk from nothing to conquer those who are opposed to its establishment, and if the foolish people from the North will only kiss the hand that smites them, and lie quietly under the heel that crushes them, he has confidence that he will restore peace and order in the territory.

What of their rights as men and as citizens? What of justice? What of squatter sovereignty? What of the honor and faith of the nation? Not one word.

The hope that constitutional liberty can be maintained in America, now rests on the integrity of the independent state governments in declaring, demanding, and securing the rights of their citizens.

It is impossible, if the policy of the new administration is to be judged from present symptoms, that the thinking citizens of each state in which men can yet afford to think freely, should not before long ask themselves:

"What are the delegated, and what the reserved rights of this state? Why should it remain in union with others for whose convenience and satisfaction its citizens are forced to relinquish, on common ground, their fundamental rights—rights, the free use of which is essential to the preservation of a decent and civilized state of society? Is it from a craven devotion to political tranquillity we allow these rights to be suppressed, systematically, formally, and year after year, and administration after administration, suppressed? Is it from pride in holding our state part of a Great Nation? Have we no patriotic duty but to keep men of our own party in office?

" What is the value of the federal constitution to us, if, in our territories, more than half our people can be deprived of the rights to which those who made the Constitution declared all men, everywhere, to be justly entitled, and which they fought a long, desperate, and bloody war to secure ?"

It is the crime of a coward and not the wisdom of a good citizen to shut his eyes to the fact, that this Union is bound straight to disastrous shipwreck, if the man at the helm maintains his present course.

The prophetic mind of Jefferson, unconsciously but clearly described the process by which we have suffered ourselves to be brought to our present perilous condition.

" Is this the kind of protection we receive in return for the rights we give up ?

" Our rulers will become corrupt, our people careless. A single zealot may commence persecutor, and better men be his victims. It can never be too often repeated that the time for fixing every essential right on a legal basis is while our rulers are honest, ourselves united. From the conclusion of this war, we shall be going down hill. It will not then be necessary to resort every moment to the people for support. They will be forgotten and their rights disregarded. They will forget themselves but in the sole faculty of making money, and will never think of uniting to effect a due respect for their rights. The shackles, therefore, which shall not be knocked off before the conclusion of this war, will remain on us long; will be made heavier and heavier till our rights shall revive or expire in a convulsion."*

"The time to guard against corruption and tyranny is before they shall have gotten hold on us. It is better to keep the wolf out of the fold, than to trust to drawing his teeth and talons, after he shall have entered."†

* Notes on Virginia. London, 1787, p. 269.
† Ibid, p. 197.